I0308998

C-4934 CAREER EXAMINATION SERIES

***This is your PASSBOOK for...***

# Workers' Compensation Analyst

***Test Preparation Study Guide***
***Questions & Answers***

NLC®

NATIONAL LEARNING CORPORATION®

**National Learning Corporation**

212 Michael Drive, Syosset, NY 11791
(516) 921-8888 • www.passbooks.com
E-mail: info@passbooks.com

# PASSBOOK® SERIES

THE *PASSBOOK® SERIES* has been created to prepare applicants and candidates for the ultimate academic battlefield – the examination room.

At some time in our lives, each and every one of us may be required to take an examination – for validation, matriculation, admission, qualification, registration, certification, or licensure.

Based on the assumption that every applicant or candidate has met the basic formal educational standards, has taken the required number of courses, and read the necessary texts, the *PASSBOOK® SERIES* furnishes the one special preparation which may assure passing with confidence, instead of failing with insecurity. Examination questions – together with answers – are furnished as the basic vehicle for study so that the mysteries of the examination and its compounding difficulties may be eliminated or diminished by a sure method.

This book is meant to help you pass your examination provided that you qualify and are serious in your objective.

The entire field is reviewed through the huge store of content information which is succinctly presented through a provocative and challenging approach – the question-and-answer method.

A climate of success is established by furnishing the correct answers at the end of each test.

You soon learn to recognize types of questions, forms of questions, and patterns of questioning. You may even begin to anticipate expected outcomes.

You perceive that many questions are repeated or adapted so that you can gain acute insights, which may enable you to score many sure points.

You learn how to confront new questions, or types of questions, and to attack them confidently and work out the correct answers.

You note objectives and emphases, and recognize pitfalls and dangers, so that you may make positive educational adjustments.

Moreover, you are kept fully informed in relation to new concepts, methods, practices, and directions in the field.

You discover that you are actually taking the examination all the time: you are preparing for the examination by "taking" an examination, not by reading extraneous and/or supererogatory textbooks.

In short, this PASSBOOK®, used directedly, should be an important factor in helping you to pass your test.

# WORKERS' COMPENSATION ANALYST

DUTIES:

A Workers' Compensation Analyst administers Workers' Compensation benefits for injured employees; authorizes appropriate treatment and assures that treatment is prompt, adequate, and economical; interviews injured employees, physicians, and witnesses and does other field investigation work; and discusses cases with attorneys, physicians, representatives of employee groups, and other persons involved in Workers' Compensation.

SCOPE OF THE EXAMINATION:

The examination will consist of a qualifying written test, an advisory essay, and an interview. In the qualifying written test, which will consist of multiple-choice questions, the following competencies may be evaluated: Judgment and Decision Making, Analytical Ability, Customer Service, Written Communication, and Job Knowledge, including knowledge of: State policies as they apply to workers' compensation benefits; mandatory benefit notices, payment methods, reimbursement requirements, collection agencies, and lien claimants; Court decisions related to matters such as injuries/illnesses incurred to and from the place of employment, employees' rights, employers' right to subrogation and apportionment; the Rules of the Workers' Compensation Appeals Board (WCAB); medical and anatomical terminology; the Permanent Disability Rating System; the Independent Medical Review (IMR), Utilization Review (UR), and Independent Bill Review (IBR) rules, regulations, and procedures as set forth by the Department of Industrial Relations Medical Unit; utilization review processes and guidelines; and other necessary skills, knowledge

# HOW TO TAKE A TEST

## I. YOU MUST PASS AN EXAMINATION

### *A. WHAT EVERY CANDIDATE SHOULD KNOW*

Examination applicants often ask us for help in preparing for the written test. What can I study in advance? What kinds of questions will be asked? How will the test be given? How will the papers be graded?

As an applicant for a civil service examination, you may be wondering about some of these things. Our purpose here is to suggest effective methods of advance study and to describe civil service examinations.

Your chances for success on this examination can be increased if you know how to prepare. Those "pre-examination jitters" can be reduced if you know what to expect. You can even experience an adventure in good citizenship if you know why civil service exams are given.

### *B. WHY ARE CIVIL SERVICE EXAMINATIONS GIVEN?*

Civil service examinations are important to you in two ways. As a citizen, you want public jobs filled by employees who know how to do their work. As a job seeker, you want a fair chance to compete for that job on an equal footing with other candidates. The best-known means of accomplishing this two-fold goal is the competitive examination.

Exams are widely publicized throughout the nation. They may be administered for jobs in federal, state, city, municipal, town or village governments or agencies.

Any citizen may apply, with some limitations, such as the age or residence of applicants. Your experience and education may be reviewed to see whether you meet the requirements for the particular examination. When these requirements exist, they are reasonable and applied consistently to all applicants. Thus, a competitive examination may cause you some uneasiness now, but it is your privilege and safeguard.

### *C. HOW ARE CIVIL SERVICE EXAMS DEVELOPED?*

Examinations are carefully written by trained technicians who are specialists in the field known as "psychological measurement," in consultation with recognized authorities in the field of work that the test will cover. These experts recommend the subject matter areas or skills to be tested; only those knowledges or skills important to your success on the job are included. The most reliable books and source materials available are used as references. Together, the experts and technicians judge the difficulty level of the questions.

Test technicians know how to phrase questions so that the problem is clearly stated. Their ethics do not permit "trick" or "catch" questions. Questions may have been tried out on sample groups, or subjected to statistical analysis, to determine their usefulness.

Written tests are often used in combination with performance tests, ratings of training and experience, and oral interviews. All of these measures combine to form the best-known means of finding the right person for the right job.

## II. HOW TO PASS THE WRITTEN TEST

### *A. NATURE OF THE EXAMINATION*

To prepare intelligently for civil service examinations, you should know how they differ from school examinations you have taken. In school you were assigned certain definite pages to read or subjects to cover. The examination questions were quite detailed and usually emphasized memory. Civil service exams, on the other hand, try to discover your present ability to perform the duties of a position, plus your potentiality to learn these duties. In other words, a civil service exam attempts to predict how successful you will be. Questions cover such a broad area that they cannot be as minute and detailed as school exam questions.

In the public service similar kinds of work, or positions, are grouped together in one "class." This process is known as *position-classification.* All the positions in a class are paid according to the salary range for that class. One class title covers all of these positions, and they are all tested by the same examination.

### *B. FOUR BASIC STEPS*

#### 1) Study the announcement

How, then, can you know what subjects to study? Our best answer is: "Learn as much as possible about the class of positions for which you've applied." The exam will test the knowledge, skills and abilities needed to do the work.

Your most valuable source of information about the position you want is the official exam announcement. This announcement lists the training and experience qualifications. Check these standards and apply only if you come reasonably close to meeting them.

The brief description of the position in the examination announcement offers some clues to the subjects which will be tested. Think about the job itself. Review the duties in your mind. Can you perform them, or are there some in which you are rusty? Fill in the blank spots in your preparation.

Many jurisdictions preview the written test in the exam announcement by including a section called "Knowledge and Abilities Required," "Scope of the Examination," or some similar heading. Here you will find out specifically what fields will be tested.

#### 2) Review your own background

Once you learn in general what the position is all about, and what you need to know to do the work, ask yourself which subjects you already know fairly well and which need improvement. You may wonder whether to concentrate on improving your strong areas or on building some background in your fields of weakness. When the announcement has specified "some knowledge" or "considerable knowledge," or has used adjectives like "beginning principles of..." or "advanced ... methods," you can get a clue as to the number and difficulty of questions to be asked in any given field. More questions, and hence broader coverage, would be included for those subjects which are more important in the work. Now weigh your strengths and weaknesses against the job requirements and prepare accordingly.

#### 3) Determine the level of the position

Another way to tell how intensively you should prepare is to understand the level of the job for which you are applying. Is it the entering level? In other words, is this the position in which beginners in a field of work are hired? Or is it an intermediate or advanced level? Sometimes this is indicated by such words as "Junior" or "Senior" in the class title. Other jurisdictions use Roman numerals to designate the level – Clerk I, Clerk II, for example. The word "Supervisor" sometimes appears in the title. If the level is not indicated by the title, check the description of duties. Will you be working under very close supervision, or will you have responsibility for independent decisions in this work?

**4) Choose appropriate study materials**

Now that you know the subjects to be examined and the relative amount of each subject to be covered, you can choose suitable study materials. For beginning level jobs, or even advanced ones, if you have a pronounced weakness in some aspect of your training, read a modern, standard textbook in that field. Be sure it is up to date and has general coverage. Such books are normally available at your library, and the librarian will be glad to help you locate one. For entry-level positions, questions of appropriate difficulty are chosen – neither highly advanced questions, nor those too simple. Such questions require careful thought but not advanced training.

If the position for which you are applying is technical or advanced, you will read more advanced, specialized material. If you are already familiar with the basic principles of your field, elementary textbooks would waste your time. Concentrate on advanced textbooks and technical periodicals. Think through the concepts and review difficult problems in your field.

These are all general sources. You can get more ideas on your own initiative, following these leads. For example, training manuals and publications of the government agency which employs workers in your field can be useful, particularly for technical and professional positions. A letter or visit to the government department involved may result in more specific study suggestions, and certainly will provide you with a more definite idea of the exact nature of the position you are seeking.

## III. KINDS OF TESTS

Tests are used for purposes other than measuring knowledge and ability to perform specified duties. For some positions, it is equally important to test ability to make adjustments to new situations or to profit from training. In others, basic mental abilities not dependent on information are essential. Questions which test these things may not appear as pertinent to the duties of the position as those which test for knowledge and information. Yet they are often highly important parts of a fair examination. For very general questions, it is almost impossible to help you direct your study efforts. What we can do is to point out some of the more common of these general abilities needed in public service positions and describe some typical questions.

1) General information

Broad, general information has been found useful for predicting job success in some kinds of work. This is tested in a variety of ways, from vocabulary lists to questions about current events. Basic background in some field of work, such as sociology or economics, may be sampled in a group of questions. Often these are principles which have become familiar to most persons through exposure rather than through formal training. It is difficult to advise you how to study for these questions; being alert to the world around you is our best suggestion.

2) Verbal ability

An example of an ability needed in many positions is verbal or language ability. Verbal ability is, in brief, the ability to use and understand words. Vocabulary and grammar tests are typical measures of this ability. Reading comprehension or paragraph interpretation questions are common in many kinds of civil service tests. You are given a paragraph of written material and asked to find its central meaning.

3) Numerical ability

Number skills can be tested by the familiar arithmetic problem, by checking paired lists of numbers to see which are alike and which are different, or by interpreting charts and graphs. In the latter test, a graph may be printed in the test booklet which you are asked to use as the basis for answering questions.

4) Observation

A popular test for law-enforcement positions is the observation test. A picture is shown to you for several minutes, then taken away. Questions about the picture test your ability to observe both details and larger elements.

5) Following directions

In many positions in the public service, the employee must be able to carry out written instructions dependably and accurately. You may be given a chart with several columns, each column listing a variety of information. The questions require you to carry out directions involving the information given in the chart.

6) Skills and aptitudes

Performance tests effectively measure some manual skills and aptitudes. When the skill is one in which you are trained, such as typing or shorthand, you can practice. These tests are often very much like those given in business school or high school courses. For many of the other skills and aptitudes, however, no short-time preparation can be made. Skills and abilities natural to you or that you have developed throughout your lifetime are being tested.

Many of the general questions just described provide all the data needed to answer the questions and ask you to use your reasoning ability to find the answers. Your best preparation for these tests, as well as for tests of facts and ideas, is to be at your physical and mental best. You, no doubt, have your own methods of getting into an exam-taking mood and keeping "in shape." The next section lists some ideas on this subject.

## IV. KINDS OF QUESTIONS

Only rarely is the "essay" question, which you answer in narrative form, used in civil service tests. Civil service tests are usually of the short-answer type. Full instructions for answering these questions will be given to you at the examination. But in case this is your first experience with short-answer questions and separate answer sheets, here is what you need to know:

### 1) Multiple-choice Questions

Most popular of the short-answer questions is the "multiple choice" or "best answer" question. It can be used, for example, to test for factual knowledge, ability to solve problems or judgment in meeting situations found at work.

A multiple-choice question is normally one of three types—

- It can begin with an incomplete statement followed by several possible endings. You are to find the one ending which *best* completes the statement, although some of the others may not be entirely wrong.
- It can also be a complete statement in the form of a question which is answered by choosing one of the statements listed.

- It can be in the form of a problem – again you select the best answer.

Here is an example of a multiple-choice question with a discussion which should give you some clues as to the method for choosing the right answer:

When an employee has a complaint about his assignment, the action which will *best* help him overcome his difficulty is to
A. discuss his difficulty with his coworkers
B. take the problem to the head of the organization
C. take the problem to the person who gave him the assignment
D. say nothing to anyone about his complaint

In answering this question, you should study each of the choices to find which is best. Consider choice "A" – Certainly an employee may discuss his complaint with fellow employees, but no change or improvement can result, and the complaint remains unresolved. Choice "B" is a poor choice since the head of the organization probably does not know what assignment you have been given, and taking your problem to him is known as "going over the head" of the supervisor. The supervisor, or person who made the assignment, is the person who can clarify it or correct any injustice. Choice "C" is, therefore, correct. To say nothing, as in choice "D," is unwise. Supervisors have and interest in knowing the problems employees are facing, and the employee is seeking a solution to his problem.

**2) True/False Questions**

The "true/false" or "right/wrong" form of question is sometimes used. Here a complete statement is given. Your job is to decide whether the statement is right or wrong.

SAMPLE: A roaming cell-phone call to a nearby city costs less than a non-roaming call to a distant city.

This statement is wrong, or false, since roaming calls are more expensive.

This is not a complete list of all possible question forms, although most of the others are variations of these common types. You will always get complete directions for answering questions. Be sure you understand *how* to mark your answers – ask questions until you do.

## V. RECORDING YOUR ANSWERS

Computer terminals are used more and more today for many different kinds of exams.

For an examination with very few applicants, you may be told to record your answers in the test booklet itself. Separate answer sheets are much more common. If this separate answer sheet is to be scored by machine – and this is often the case – it is highly important that you mark your answers correctly in order to get credit.

An electronic scoring machine is often used in civil service offices because of the speed with which papers can be scored. Machine-scored answer sheets must be marked with a pencil, which will be given to you. This pencil has a high graphite content which responds to the electronic scoring machine. As a matter of fact, stray dots may register as answers, so do not let your pencil rest on the answer sheet while you are pondering the correct answer. Also, if your pencil lead breaks or is otherwise defective, ask for another.

Since the answer sheet will be dropped in a slot in the scoring machine, be careful not to bend the corners or get the paper crumpled.

The answer sheet normally has five vertical columns of numbers, with 30 numbers to a column. These numbers correspond to the question numbers in your test booklet. After each number, going across the page are four or five pairs of dotted lines. These short dotted lines have small letters or numbers above them. The first two pairs may also have a "T" or "F" above the letters. This indicates that the first two pairs only are to be used if the questions are of the true-false type. If the questions are multiple choice, disregard the "T" and "F" and pay attention only to the small letters or numbers.

Answer your questions in the manner of the sample that follows:

32. The largest city in the United States is
    A. Washington, D.C.
    B. New York City
    C. Chicago
    D. Detroit
    E. San Francisco

1) Choose the answer you think is best. (New York City is the largest, so "B" is correct.)
2) Find the row of dotted lines numbered the same as the question you are answering. (Find row number 32)
3) Find the pair of dotted lines corresponding to the answer. (Find the pair of lines under the mark "B.")
4) Make a solid black mark between the dotted lines.

## VI. BEFORE THE TEST

Common sense will help you find procedures to follow to get ready for an examination. Too many of us, however, overlook these sensible measures. Indeed, nervousness and fatigue have been found to be the most serious reasons why applicants fail to do their best on civil service tests. Here is a list of reminders:

- Begin your preparation early – Don't wait until the last minute to go scurrying around for books and materials or to find out what the position is all about.
- Prepare continuously – An hour a night for a week is better than an all-night cram session. This has been definitely established. What is more, a night a week for a month will return better dividends than crowding your study into a shorter period of time.
- Locate the place of the exam – You have been sent a notice telling you when and where to report for the examination. If the location is in a different town or otherwise unfamiliar to you, it would be well to inquire the best route and learn something about the building.
- Relax the night before the test – Allow your mind to rest. Do not study at all that night. Plan some mild recreation or diversion; then go to bed early and get a good night's sleep.
- Get up early enough to make a leisurely trip to the place for the test – This way unforeseen events, traffic snarls, unfamiliar buildings, etc. will not upset you.
- Dress comfortably – A written test is not a fashion show. You will be known by number and not by name, so wear something comfortable.

- Leave excess paraphernalia at home – Shopping bags and odd bundles will get in your way. You need bring only the items mentioned in the official notice you received; usually everything you need is provided. Do not bring reference books to the exam. They will only confuse those last minutes and be taken away from you when in the test room.
- Arrive somewhat ahead of time – If because of transportation schedules you must get there very early, bring a newspaper or magazine to take your mind off yourself while waiting.
- Locate the examination room – When you have found the proper room, you will be directed to the seat or part of the room where you will sit. Sometimes you are given a sheet of instructions to read while you are waiting. Do not fill out any forms until you are told to do so; just read them and be prepared.
- Relax and prepare to listen to the instructions
- If you have any physical problem that may keep you from doing your best, be sure to tell the test administrator. If you are sick or in poor health, you really cannot do your best on the exam. You can come back and take the test some other time.

## VII. AT THE TEST

The day of the test is here and you have the test booklet in your hand. The temptation to get going is very strong. Caution! There is more to success than knowing the right answers. You must know how to identify your papers and understand variations in the type of short-answer question used in this particular examination. Follow these suggestions for maximum results from your efforts:

**1) Cooperate with the monitor**

The test administrator has a duty to create a situation in which you can be as much at ease as possible. He will give instructions, tell you when to begin, check to see that you are marking your answer sheet correctly, and so on. He is not there to guard you, although he will see that your competitors do not take unfair advantage. He wants to help you do your best.

**2) Listen to all instructions**

Don't jump the gun! Wait until you understand all directions. In most civil service tests you get more time than you need to answer the questions. So don't be in a hurry. Read each word of instructions until you clearly understand the meaning. Study the examples, listen to all announcements and follow directions. Ask questions if you do not understand what to do.

**3) Identify your papers**

Civil service exams are usually identified by number only. You will be assigned a number; you must not put your name on your test papers. Be sure to copy your number correctly. Since more than one exam may be given, copy your exact examination title.

**4) Plan your time**

Unless you are told that a test is a "speed" or "rate of work" test, speed itself is usually not important. Time enough to answer all the questions will be provided, but this does not mean that you have all day. An overall time limit has been set. Divide the total time (in minutes) by the number of questions to determine the approximate time you have for each question.

**5) Do not linger over difficult questions**

If you come across a difficult question, mark it with a paper clip (useful to have along) and come back to it when you have been through the booklet. One caution if you do this – be sure to skip a number on your answer sheet as well. Check often to be sure that you have not lost your place and that you are marking in the row numbered the same as the question you are answering.

**6) Read the questions**

Be sure you know what the question asks! Many capable people are unsuccessful because they failed to *read* the questions correctly.

**7) Answer all questions**

Unless you have been instructed that a penalty will be deducted for incorrect answers, it is better to guess than to omit a question.

**8) Speed tests**

It is often better NOT to guess on speed tests. It has been found that on timed tests people are tempted to spend the last few seconds before time is called in marking answers at random – without even reading them – in the hope of picking up a few extra points. To discourage this practice, the instructions may warn you that your score will be "corrected" for guessing. That is, a penalty will be applied. The incorrect answers will be deducted from the correct ones, or some other penalty formula will be used.

**9) Review your answers**

If you finish before time is called, go back to the questions you guessed or omitted to give them further thought. Review other answers if you have time.

**10) Return your test materials**

If you are ready to leave before others have finished or time is called, take ALL your materials to the monitor and leave quietly. Never take any test material with you. The monitor can discover whose papers are not complete, and taking a test booklet may be grounds for disqualification.

## VIII. EXAMINATION TECHNIQUES

1) Read the general instructions carefully. These are usually printed on the first page of the exam booklet. As a rule, these instructions refer to the timing of the examination; the fact that you should not start work until the signal and must stop work at a signal, etc. If there are any *special* instructions, such as a choice of questions to be answered, make sure that you note this instruction carefully.

2) When you are ready to start work on the examination, that is as soon as the signal has been given, read the instructions to each question booklet, underline any key words or phrases, such as *least, best, outline, describe* and the like. In this way you will tend to answer as requested rather than discover on reviewing your paper that you *listed without describing*, that you selected the *worst* choice rather than the *best* choice, etc.

3) If the examination is of the objective or multiple-choice type – that is, each question will also give a series of possible answers: A, B, C or D, and you are called upon to select the best answer and write the letter next to that answer on your answer paper – it is advisable to start answering each question in turn. There may be anywhere from 50 to 100 such questions in the three or four hours allotted and you can see how much time would be taken if you read through all the questions before beginning to answer any. Furthermore, if you come across a question or group of questions which you know would be difficult to answer, it would undoubtedly affect your handling of all the other questions.

4) If the examination is of the essay type and contains but a few questions, it is a moot point as to whether you should read all the questions before starting to answer any one. Of course, if you are given a choice – say five out of seven and the like – then it is essential to read all the questions so you can eliminate the two that are most difficult. If, however, you are asked to answer all the questions, there may be danger in trying to answer the easiest one first because you may find that you will spend too much time on it. The best technique is to answer the first question, then proceed to the second, etc.

5) Time your answers. Before the exam begins, write down the time it started, then add the time allowed for the examination and write down the time it must be completed, then divide the time available somewhat as follows:
   - If 3-1/2 hours are allowed, that would be 210 minutes. If you have 80 objective-type questions, that would be an average of 2-1/2 minutes per question. Allow yourself no more than 2 minutes per question, or a total of 160 minutes, which will permit about 50 minutes to review.
   - If for the time allotment of 210 minutes there are 7 essay questions to answer, that would average about 30 minutes a question. Give yourself only 25 minutes per question so that you have about 35 minutes to review.

6) The most important instruction is to *read each question* and make sure you know what is wanted. The second most important instruction is to *time yourself properly* so that you answer every question. The third most important instruction is to *answer every question.* Guess if you have to but include something for each question. Remember that you will receive no credit for a blank and will probably receive some credit if you write something in answer to an essay question. If you guess a letter – say "B" for a multiple-choice question – you may have guessed right. If you leave a blank as an answer to a multiple-choice question, the examiners may respect your feelings but it will not add a point to your score. Some exams may penalize you for wrong answers, so in such cases *only*, you may not want to guess unless you have some basis for your answer.

7) Suggestions
   a. Objective-type questions
      1. Examine the question booklet for proper sequence of pages and questions
      2. Read all instructions carefully
      3. Skip any question which seems too difficult; return to it after all other questions have been answered
      4. Apportion your time properly; do not spend too much time on any single question or group of questions

5. Note and underline key words – *all, most, fewest, least, best, worst, same, opposite,* etc.
6. Pay particular attention to negatives
7. Note unusual option, e.g., unduly long, short, complex, different or similar in content to the body of the question
8. Observe the use of "hedging" words – *probably, may, most likely,* etc.
9. Make sure that your answer is put next to the same number as the question
10. Do not second-guess unless you have good reason to believe the second answer is definitely more correct
11. Cross out original answer if you decide another answer is more accurate; do not erase until you are ready to hand your paper in
12. Answer all questions; guess unless instructed otherwise
13. Leave time for review

b. Essay questions
   1. Read each question carefully
   2. Determine exactly what is wanted. Underline key words or phrases.
   3. Decide on outline or paragraph answer
   4. Include many different points and elements unless asked to develop any one or two points or elements
   5. Show impartiality by giving pros and cons unless directed to select one side only
   6. Make and write down any assumptions you find necessary to answer the questions
   7. Watch your English, grammar, punctuation and choice of words
   8. Time your answers; don't crowd material

8) Answering the essay question

Most essay questions can be answered by framing the specific response around several key words or ideas. Here are a few such key words or ideas:

M's: manpower, materials, methods, money, management
P's: purpose, program, policy, plan, procedure, practice, problems, pitfalls, personnel, public relations

a. Six basic steps in handling problems:
   1. Preliminary plan and background development
   2. Collect information, data and facts
   3. Analyze and interpret information, data and facts
   4. Analyze and develop solutions as well as make recommendations
   5. Prepare report and sell recommendations
   6. Install recommendations and follow up effectiveness

b. Pitfalls to avoid
   1. *Taking things for granted* – A statement of the situation does not necessarily imply that each of the elements is necessarily true; for example, a complaint may be invalid and biased so that all that can be taken for granted is that a complaint has been registered

2. *Considering only one side of a situation* – Wherever possible, indicate several alternatives and then point out the reasons you selected the best one
3. *Failing to indicate follow up* – Whenever your answer indicates action on your part, make certain that you will take proper follow-up action to see how successful your recommendations, procedures or actions turn out to be
4. *Taking too long in answering any single question* – Remember to time your answers properly

## IX. AFTER THE TEST

Scoring procedures differ in detail among civil service jurisdictions although the general principles are the same. Whether the papers are hand-scored or graded by machine we have described, they are nearly always graded by number. That is, the person who marks the paper knows only the number – never the name – of the applicant. Not until all the papers have been graded will they be matched with names. If other tests, such as training and experience or oral interview ratings have been given, scores will be combined. Different parts of the examination usually have different weights. For example, the written test might count 60 percent of the final grade, and a rating of training and experience 40 percent. In many jurisdictions, veterans will have a certain number of points added to their grades.

After the final grade has been determined, the names are placed in grade order and an eligible list is established. There are various methods for resolving ties between those who get the same final grade – probably the most common is to place first the name of the person whose application was received first. Job offers are made from the eligible list in the order the names appear on it. You will be notified of your grade and your rank as soon as all these computations have been made. This will be done as rapidly as possible.

People who are found to meet the requirements in the announcement are called "eligibles." Their names are put on a list of eligible candidates. An eligible's chances of getting a job depend on how high he stands on this list and how fast agencies are filling jobs from the list.

When a job is to be filled from a list of eligibles, the agency asks for the names of people on the list of eligibles for that job. When the civil service commission receives this request, it sends to the agency the names of the three people highest on this list. Or, if the job to be filled has specialized requirements, the office sends the agency the names of the top three persons who meet these requirements from the general list.

The appointing officer makes a choice from among the three people whose names were sent to him. If the selected person accepts the appointment, the names of the others are put back on the list to be considered for future openings.

That is the rule in hiring from all kinds of eligible lists, whether they are for typist, carpenter, chemist, or something else. For every vacancy, the appointing officer has his choice of any one of the top three eligibles on the list. This explains why the person whose name is on top of the list sometimes does not get an appointment when some of the persons lower on the list do. If the appointing officer chooses the second or third eligible, the No. 1 eligible does not get a job at once, but stays on the list until he is appointed or the list is terminated.

## X. HOW TO PASS THE INTERVIEW TEST

The examination for which you applied requires an oral interview test. You have already taken the written test and you are now being called for the interview test – the final part of the formal examination.

You may think that it is not possible to prepare for an interview test and that there are no procedures to follow during an interview. Our purpose is to point out some things you can do in advance that will help you and some good rules to follow and pitfalls to avoid while you are being interviewed.

*What is an interview supposed to test?*

The written examination is designed to test the technical knowledge and competence of the candidate; the oral is designed to evaluate intangible qualities, not readily measured otherwise, and to establish a list showing the relative fitness of each candidate – as measured against his competitors – for the position sought. Scoring is not on the basis of "right" and "wrong," but on a sliding scale of values ranging from "not passable" to "outstanding." As a matter of fact, it is possible to achieve a relatively low score without a single "incorrect" answer because of evident weakness in the qualities being measured.

Occasionally, an examination may consist entirely of an oral test – either an individual or a group oral. In such cases, information is sought concerning the technical knowledges and abilities of the candidate, since there has been no written examination for this purpose. More commonly, however, an oral test is used to supplement a written examination.

*Who conducts interviews?*

The composition of oral boards varies among different jurisdictions. In nearly all, a representative of the personnel department serves as chairman. One of the members of the board may be a representative of the department in which the candidate would work. In some cases, "outside experts" are used, and, frequently, a businessman or some other representative of the general public is asked to serve. Labor and management or other special groups may be represented. The aim is to secure the services of experts in the appropriate field.

However the board is composed, it is a good idea (and not at all improper or unethical) to ascertain in advance of the interview who the members are and what groups they represent. When you are introduced to them, you will have some idea of their backgrounds and interests, and at least you will not stutter and stammer over their names.

*What should be done before the interview?*

While knowledge about the board members is useful and takes some of the surprise element out of the interview, there is other preparation which is more substantive. It *is* possible to prepare for an oral interview – in several ways:

**1) Keep a copy of your application and review it carefully before the interview**

This may be the only document before the oral board, and the starting point of the interview. Know what education and experience you have listed there, and the sequence and dates of all of it. Sometimes the board will ask you to review the highlights of your experience for them; you should not have to hem and haw doing it.

**2) Study the class specification and the examination announcement**

Usually, the oral board has one or both of these to guide them. The qualities, characteristics or knowledges required by the position sought are stated in these documents. They offer valuable clues as to the nature of the oral interview. For example, if the job involves supervisory responsibilities, the announcement will usually indicate that knowledge of modern supervisory methods and the qualifications of the candidate as a supervisor will be tested. If so, you can expect such questions, frequently in the form of a hypothetical situation which you are expected to solve. NEVER go into an oral without knowledge of the duties and responsibilities of the job you seek.

**3) Think through each qualification required**

Try to visualize the kind of questions you would ask if you were a board member. How well could you answer them? Try especially to appraise your own knowledge and background in each area, *measured against the job sought*, and identify any areas in which you are weak. Be critical and realistic – do not flatter yourself.

**4) Do some general reading in areas in which you feel you may be weak**

For example, if the job involves supervision and your past experience has NOT, some general reading in supervisory methods and practices, particularly in the field of human relations, might be useful. Do NOT study agency procedures or detailed manuals. The oral board will be testing your understanding and capacity, not your memory.

**5) Get a good night's sleep and watch your general health and mental attitude**

You will want a clear head at the interview. Take care of a cold or any other minor ailment, and of course, no hangovers.

*What should be done on the day of the interview?*

Now comes the day of the interview itself. Give yourself plenty of time to get there. Plan to arrive somewhat ahead of the scheduled time, particularly if your appointment is in the fore part of the day. If a previous candidate fails to appear, the board might be ready for you a bit early. By early afternoon an oral board is almost invariably behind schedule if there are many candidates, and you may have to wait. Take along a book or magazine to read, or your application to review, but leave any extraneous material in the waiting room when you go in for your interview. In any event, relax and compose yourself.

The matter of dress is important. The board is forming impressions about you – from your experience, your manners, your attitude, and your appearance. Give your personal appearance careful attention. Dress your best, but not your flashiest. Choose conservative, appropriate clothing, and be sure it is immaculate. This is a business interview, and your appearance should indicate that you regard it as such. Besides, being well groomed and properly dressed will help boost your confidence.

Sooner or later, someone will call your name and escort you into the interview room. *This is it.* From here on you are on your own. It is too late for any more preparation. But remember, you asked for this opportunity to prove your fitness, and you are here because your request was granted.

*What happens when you go in?*

The usual sequence of events will be as follows: The clerk (who is often the board stenographer) will introduce you to the chairman of the oral board, who will introduce you to the other members of the board. Acknowledge the introductions before you sit down. Do not be surprised if you find a microphone facing you or a stenotypist sitting by. Oral interviews are usually recorded in the event of an appeal or other review.

Usually the chairman of the board will open the interview by reviewing the highlights of your education and work experience from your application – primarily for the benefit of the other members of the board, as well as to get the material into the record. Do not interrupt or comment unless there is an error or significant misinterpretation; if that is the case, do not hesitate. But do not quibble about insignificant matters. Also, he will usually ask you some question about your education, experience or your present job – partly to get you to start talking and to establish the interviewing "rapport." He may start the actual questioning, or turn it over to one of the other members. Frequently, each member undertakes the questioning on a particular area, one in which he is perhaps most competent, so you can expect each member to participate in the examination. Because time is limited, you may also expect some rather abrupt switches in the direction the questioning takes, so do not be upset by it. Normally, a board member will not pursue a single line of questioning unless he discovers a particular strength or weakness.

After each member has participated, the chairman will usually ask whether any member has any further questions, then will ask you if you have anything you wish to add. Unless you are expecting this question, it may floor you. Worse, it may start you off on an extended, extemporaneous speech. The board is not usually seeking more information. The question is principally to offer you a last opportunity to present further qualifications or to indicate that you have nothing to add. So, if you feel that a significant qualification or characteristic has been overlooked, it is proper to point it out in a sentence or so. Do not compliment the board on the thoroughness of their examination – they have been sketchy, and you know it. If you wish, merely say, "No thank you, I have nothing further to add." This is a point where you can "talk yourself out" of a good impression or fail to present an important bit of information. Remember, *you close the interview yourself.*

The chairman will then say, "That is all, Mr. _______, thank you." Do not be startled; the interview is over, and quicker than you think. Thank him, gather your belongings and take your leave. Save your sigh of relief for the other side of the door.

*How to put your best foot forward*

Throughout this entire process, you may feel that the board individually and collectively is trying to pierce your defenses, seek out your hidden weaknesses and embarrass and confuse you. Actually, this is not true. They are obliged to make an appraisal of your qualifications for the job you are seeking, and they want to see you in your best light. Remember, they must interview all candidates and a non-cooperative candidate may become a failure in spite of their best efforts to bring out his qualifications. Here are 15 suggestions that will help you:

**1) Be natural – Keep your attitude confident, not cocky**

If you are not confident that you can do the job, do not expect the board to be. Do not apologize for your weaknesses, try to bring out your strong points. The board is interested in a positive, not negative, presentation. Cockiness will antagonize any board member and make him wonder if you are covering up a weakness by a false show of strength.

**2) Get comfortable, but don't lounge or sprawl**

Sit erectly but not stiffly. A careless posture may lead the board to conclude that you are careless in other things, or at least that you are not impressed by the importance of the occasion. Either conclusion is natural, even if incorrect. Do not fuss with your clothing, a pencil or an ashtray. Your hands may occasionally be useful to emphasize a point; do not let them become a point of distraction.

**3) Do not wisecrack or make small talk**

This is a serious situation, and your attitude should show that you consider it as such. Further, the time of the board is limited – they do not want to waste it, and neither should you.

**4) Do not exaggerate your experience or abilities**

In the first place, from information in the application or other interviews and sources, the board may know more about you than you think. Secondly, you probably will not get away with it. An experienced board is rather adept at spotting such a situation, so do not take the chance.

**5) If you know a board member, do not make a point of it, yet do not hide it**

Certainly you are not fooling him, and probably not the other members of the board. Do not try to take advantage of your acquaintanceship – it will probably do you little good.

**6) Do not dominate the interview**

Let the board do that. They will give you the clues – do not assume that you have to do all the talking. Realize that the board has a number of questions to ask you, and do not try to take up all the interview time by showing off your extensive knowledge of the answer to the first one.

**7) Be attentive**

You only have 20 minutes or so, and you should keep your attention at its sharpest throughout. When a member is addressing a problem or question to you, give him your undivided attention. Address your reply principally to him, but do not exclude the other board members.

**8) Do not interrupt**

A board member may be stating a problem for you to analyze. He will ask you a question when the time comes. Let him state the problem, and wait for the question.

**9) Make sure you understand the question**

Do not try to answer until you are sure what the question is. If it is not clear, restate it in your own words or ask the board member to clarify it for you. However, do not haggle about minor elements.

**10) Reply promptly but not hastily**

A common entry on oral board rating sheets is "candidate responded readily," or "candidate hesitated in replies." Respond as promptly and quickly as you can, but do not jump to a hasty, ill-considered answer.

**11) Do not be peremptory in your answers**

A brief answer is proper – but do not fire your answer back. That is a losing game from your point of view. The board member can probably ask questions much faster than you can answer them.

**12) Do not try to create the answer you think the board member wants**

He is interested in what kind of mind you have and how it works – not in playing games. Furthermore, he can usually spot this practice and will actually grade you down on it.

**13) Do not switch sides in your reply merely to agree with a board member**

Frequently, a member will take a contrary position merely to draw you out and to see if you are willing and able to defend your point of view. Do not start a debate, yet do not surrender a good position. If a position is worth taking, it is worth defending.

**14) Do not be afraid to admit an error in judgment if you are shown to be wrong**

The board knows that you are forced to reply without any opportunity for careful consideration. Your answer may be demonstrably wrong. If so, admit it and get on with the interview.

**15) Do not dwell at length on your present job**

The opening question may relate to your present assignment. Answer the question but do not go into an extended discussion. You are being examined for a *new* job, not your present one. As a matter of fact, try to phrase ALL your answers in terms of the job for which you are being examined.

*Basis of Rating*

Probably you will forget most of these "do's" and "don'ts" when you walk into the oral interview room. Even remembering them all will not ensure you a passing grade. Perhaps you did not have the qualifications in the first place. But remembering them will help you to put your best foot forward, without treading on the toes of the board members.

Rumor and popular opinion to the contrary notwithstanding, an oral board wants you to make the best appearance possible. They know you are under pressure – but they also want to see how you respond to it as a guide to what your reaction would be under the pressures of the job you seek. They will be influenced by the degree of poise you display, the personal traits you show and the manner in which you respond.

ABOUT THIS BOOK

This book contains tests divided into Examination Sections. Go through each test, answering every question in the margin. We have also attached a sample answer sheet at the back of the book that can be removed and used. At the end of each test look at the answer key and check your answers. On the ones you got wrong, look at the right answer choice and learn. Do not fill in the answers first. Do not memorize the questions and answers, but understand the answer and principles involved. On your test, the questions will likely be different from the samples. Questions are changed and new ones added. If you understand these past questions you should have success with any changes that arise. Tests may consist of several types of questions. We have additional books on each subject should more study be advisable or necessary for you. Finally, the more you study, the better prepared you will be. This book is intended to be the last thing you study before you walk into the examination room. Prior study of relevant texts is also recommended. NLC publishes some of these in our Fundamental Series. Knowledge and good sense are important factors in passing your exam. Good luck also helps. So now study this Passbook, absorb the material contained within and take that knowledge into the examination. Then do your best to pass that exam.

---

# EXAMINATION SECTION

# EXAMINATION SECTION
# TEST 1

DIRECTIONS: Each question or incomplete statement is followed by several suggested answers or completions. Select the one that BEST answers the question or completes the statement. *PRINT THE LETTER OF THE CORRECT ANSWER IN THE SPACE AT THE RIGHT.*

1. The following passage is taken from the Workers' Compensation Provisions of the Consolidated Laws of New York State: 1.____
*§ 238. Payments to minors. Minors shall be deemed to be sui juris for the purpose of receiving payment of benefits under this article.*
This passage means that minor employees

   A. are a unique class of employees whose cases should be considered using a different set of standards
   B. must be represented by a parent or guardian in workers' compensation cases
   C. will be compensated in the same way as any other worker who is eligible for workers' compensation
   D. must designate an adult who will nominally receive benefits and then transfer them to the minor

2. The purpose of a partial disability benefit is to 2.____

   A. allow the insured to collect full benefits during rehabilitation
   B. protect the insurer against material misrepresentation
   C. protect the insurer against adverse selection
   D. provide reduced monthly indemnity in proportion to the insured's loss of income when he/she has returned to work at reduced earnings

3. Fred has been totally disabled by a work-related injury for 415 weeks. Fred's injury has been identified as a 32 percent whole-body impairment. Under the workers' compensation system, the maximum benefit rate is .6667. Fred's average weekly wage is $378.80. The total amount of benefits received by Fred over the 415-week period is about 3.____

   A. $33,538
   B. $50,305
   C. $104,808
   D. $157,202

4. When a workers' compensation case has been refilled, with a notation that an examiner is to review the case by a specified future date, the case has said to be in 4.____

   A. apportionment
   B. abeyance
   C. reopening
   D. escrow

5. A worker has been continuously disabled for more than two years. Under many private or self-insurance plans, the insurer can request proof of continued disability no more frequently than once every 5.____

A. three years
B. eighteen months
C. six months
D. 90 days

6. An employee injured while traveling to or from work is generally NOT covered by workers compensation if he 6.___
I. is simply driving to or from the workplace
II. engages in a work-related task during the trip to or from work
III. is paid for travel time
IV. is provided transportation by the employer

A. I only
B. I or II
C. II or III
D. I, II, III or IV

7. Which of the following would LEAST likely be considered a work-related injury under federal guidelines? 7.___

A. Sharon, a data entry clerk, falls when getting out of her car before beginning work.
B. John, a chef, slips and falls while at work in the kitchen.
C. Cliff, a custodial worker, is stung by a yellowjacket in the maintenance yard and has an allergic reaction.
D. Mary, a salesperson, is injured in a car accident on her way to see her employer's client as part of her regular duties.

8. The indemnity for total disability generally is written on a ______. 8.___

A. service
B. flat
C. reimbursement
D. valued

9. The first part of a disability rating is the 9.___

A. impairment number
B. impairment standard
C. occupational grouping
D. age adjustment

10. Each of the following is a condition that constitutes presumptive disability, EXCEPT: 10.___

A. loss of the use of any limb
B. loss of sight in both eyes
C. loss of hearing in both ears
D. the loss of power of speech

11. When an employee is judged by a physician to have attained maximum medical improvement (MMI), he or she 11.____

I. is no longer eligible for workers' compensation benefits
II. has recovered from the work injury to the greatest extent that is expected
III. expects no further change in his or her condition
IV. is automatically considered to be partially disabled

A. I only
B. I and II
C. II and III
D. I, II, III and IV

12. Customer service at any agency is a matter of both style and substance. The "substance" of customer service at a workers compensation division or department would include each of the following, EXCEPT 12.____

A. friendliness and approachability
B. problem-solving skills
C. knowledge of state laws and regulations
D. knowledge about agency procedures

13. The federal ______ assigns private employers the duty to provide a workplace free of hazards that may cause death or serious harm. 13.____

A. Fair Labor Standards
B. Occupational Safety and Health
C. Employees' Compensation
D. Robinson-Patman

14. Under the ADA, employers may be required to make changes in the workplace or to a job description in response to the needs of an otherwise qualified employee or candidate with a disability. These changes are referred to as 14.____

A. rehabilitative employment
B. work modification
C. accessibility measures
D. reasonable accommodations

Questions 15 and 16 are based on the information below:

In certain industrial categories, a state workers' compensation system uses a tiered benefit system, calculating total disability benefits according to an employee's years of service at the time a disability due to illness or injury begins. An employee with 10 or more years of service receives 100 percent of his or her base salary, for up to 26 weeks. An employee with fewer than 10 years of service receives 100 percent of his or her base salary for up to the first 4 weeks (28 days). After those first four weeks, the benefit drops to 90 percent for up to the next 9 weeks (63 days); and after that the benefit is 75 percent for up to the next 13 weeks (91 days).
Ruth Brynner, who is covered under this provision, has worked at the same company for 8 years. She is injured on the job and is totally disabled, unable to return to work for 3 months, or 12 weeks. Her base salary at the time she was injured was $65,000 per year (52 weeks).

15. The total amount of benefits received by Ruth Brynner during her 4 months of total disability was 15.____

A. $12,000
B. $13,500
C. $14,000
D. $15,000

16. Gerald Simpson, who is also covered under the above provisions, has worked at the same company for five years. He is injured on the job, totally disabled, and unable to return to work for 6 months, or 24 weeks. His base salary at the time of his injury was $52,000 per year. 16.___
The total amount of benefits earned by Gerald Simpson during his 6 months of total disability was

A. $18,000
B. $20,350
C. $21,250
D. $24,000

17. Workers compensation benefits generally include payments for 17.___
I. lost wages/lost time
II. medical services
III. rehabilitation services
IV. death benefits

A. I and II
B. I, II and IV
C. I and IV
D. I, II, III and IV

18. Many workers' compensation insurers adjust premiums by adding loss reserves for estimated future claims costs to paid losses. This is a concept known as ______. 18.___

A. indirect
B. partial
C. earned
D. incurred

19. ______ are NOT typically covered under workers' compensation laws. 19.___

A. Service
B. Industrial
C. Government
D. Agricultural

20. Tim works twenty hours a week at Acme Leasing at $8 an hour, and works twenty hours a week for Bob's Country Bunker at $10) an hour. Tim is injured while working for Acme leasing. Tim's average weekly wage is calculated by multiplying the total number of hours he works in a five-day work week, regardless of his employer, by the wage he was paid at the job at which he was injured. 20.___
Tim's average weekly wage is

A. $160
B. $200

C. $320
D. $400

21. According to the U.S. Chamber of Commerce, six basic objectives underlie workers' compensation laws. Which of the following is NOT one of them? 21.____

A. To discourage injured workers from returning to work to soon after they have suffered an injury or illness.
B. To provide a single remedy that reduces court delays, costs and workloads arising from personal injury litigation.
C. To encourage maximum employer interest in safety and rehabilitation through experience-rating mechanisms.
D. To relieve public and private charities of financial drains incident to uncompensated industrial accidents.

22. In the state where Bob works, employees are entitled to workers' compensation benefits up to two-thirds of their average weekly wage, within the minimum and maximum amounts allowed by law. Bob is injured at work on June 5, 2007, and is assigned a 50 percent disability rating. The maximum average weekly amount allowed for an injury occurring in 2007 is $180 for a partial disability rating under 15 percent; $220 for a PD rating from 15 to 24.75 percent; $250 for a PD rating from 25 to 69.75 percent; and $280 for a PD rating of 70 percent or higher. Bob's average weekly wage at his job is $600. He is entitled to a maximum benefit amount of 22.____

A. $250
B. $280
C. $400
D. $600

23. Which of the following is an occupational disease that is caused by continuous trauma? 23.____

A. Chemical burn
B. Radiation sickness
C. Carpal-tunnel syndrome
D. Silicosis

24. Steve Stephens is a clerk for the U.S. Postal Service. One day at the office, Steve opens the top drawer of a filing cabinet, and the entire cabinet suddenly falls over on top of him. His left arm is broken, as well as several bones in his left foot. Which of the following describes the mechanism by which Steve can recover benefits for his injuries? 24.____

A. Steve will receive payment for his lost time and medical expenses under the Non-appropriated Fund Instrumentalities Act.
B. The Federal Employers' Liability Act allows Steve to sue his employer if his injuries resulted from the employer's negligence.
C. Steve will receive payment for his lost time and medical expenses under the state workers' compensation system
D. The Federal Employees' Compensation Act entitles Steve to receive workers' compensation benefits.

25. If a worker is partially disabled, the benefit is payable as follows: 25.____

$$\frac{A - B}{A} \times \text{weekly benefit for total disability}$$

where:
A = the worker's pre-claim weekly earnings
B = the worker's weekly earnings for work in which partial disability is claimed

Apply this formula to the following problem: Jared Hass's salary is $40,000 annually. After six years of service to Clomp Corporation, Hass is injured on the job and becomes totally disabled, earning a weekly benefit that is 75 percent of his previous salary. After several weeks, Hass returns to work on a part-time basis, earning $250 a week. His partial disability benefit will be about

A. $154
B. $250
C. $389
D. $519

# KEY (CORRECT ANSWERS)

1. C
2. D
3. A
4. B
5. C
6. A
7. A
8. D
9. A
10. A
11. C
12. A
13. B
14. D
15. C
16. B
17. D
18. D
19. D
20. C
21. A
22. A
23. C
24. D
25. C

# TEST 2

DIRECTIONS: Each question or incomplete statement is followed by several suggested answers or completions. Select the one that BEST answers the question or completes the statement. *PRINT THE LETTER OF THE CORRECT ANSWER IN THE SPACE AT THE RIGHT.*

Questions 1 and 2 refer to the information below:

In the state where Edna works, partial dependents are entitled to death benefits-four times the amount annually devoted to their respective levels of support by the deceased employee. The total benefit divided by the partial dependents, however, cannot exceed $125,000; if it does, the dependents will divide a proportionate share of the maximum.

Edna partially supported her three college-aged children: Matt received $15,000 a year from her; Carl received $7,000 annually, and Dorothy received $5,000. Edna was killed in an injury at work in October of 2000.

1. What was the death benefit received by Carl? 1.____

   A. $7,000
   B. $28,000
   C. $32,500
   D. $65,000

2. What was the total benefit received by Edna's children? 2.____

   A. $65,000
   B. $94,000
   C. $108,000
   D. $125,000

3. Questions of work-relatedness arise in situations where an employee is injured while attending to personal matters on company time. In terms of a compensation claim's validity, the most important factor to consider in these situations would be 3.____

   A. whether the employer had a suited policy of allowing employees to engage in personal activities while on the job
   B. whether the employer was aware that the employee was attending to personal matters on company time
   C. whether the employee had "punched in" for the day
   D. whether the personal matter could have been considered an emergency

4. Of the following, the most common cause of workers' compensation overcharge is 4.____

   A. incorrect scheduling of injury
   B. claimant fraud
   C. incorrect job classification code
   D. employer fraud

5. Generally, employees covered by workers compensation may not sue employers for injuries suffered in the course of their employment. Possible exceptions to this rule would include the case of 5.____
   I. John, who is assaulted by his employer during a disagreement
   II. Mary, who is injured while a passenger in her employer's car on a sales call. The accident is found largely to have been caused by the employer's speed, which was in excess of 100 miles per hour.
   III. Hank, who is injured on the job but believes his job has been misclassified by his employer in order to avoid a higher pre mium.
   IV. Ellen, a delivery assistant who is injured in the course of a delivery when a truck driven by her employer rearends the car in front of it

   A. I and II
   B. I, II, and III
   C. I and IV
   D. I, II, III and IV

6. Jerry does data entry at a computer terminal all day long. He notices pain in his right wrist and sees his family doctor, who does some testing. Jerry's doctor tells him that he has carpal tunnel syndrome, caused by his constant typing at the computer terminal at work. Jerry continues to work for another three months before finally telling his supervisor he can't work any more because of the caipal tunnel syndrome and going home. In his state, Jerry has one year from the "date of injury" to file a workers' compensation claim. For this purpose, the "date of injury" would be the day 6.____

   A. Jerry first felt pain in his right wrist
   B. the pain in Jerry's right wrist affected his work productivity
   C. Jerry's doctor told him he had carpal tunnel syndrome due to work
   D. Jerry informed his employer of the doctor's diagnosis and took off work

7. The requirements for a valid workers' compensation claim in most jurisdictions state that in order for an injury to be compensable, it must occur 7.____
   I. when the employee is actively engaged in his job
   II. while the employee is fulfilling work duties
   III. within the precise work hours prescribed by the employer.
   IV. in a location where it is reasonable for the employee to be while working

   A. I and III
   B. II and IV
   C. II, III and IV
   D. I, II, III and IV

8. Typically, partial disability is NOT 8.____

   A. insured so that benefits will encourage the insured to return to work on a limited basis during the convalescent period
   B. a condition that follows a period of total disability, if sickness is the cause
   C. defined as the inability to perform one or more important duties of the insured's regular occupation
   D. awarded the same amount as a total disability, but for a shorter period of time

9. Which of the following accurately describes a factor that affects the length of a temporary disability? 9.____

A. Blue collar workers, because of their strong cultural work ethic, tend to have relatively shorter periods of temporary disability.
B. Younger workers, because of their lack of caution, tend to suffer injuries that take longer to heal.
C. The claimant may be motivated to prolong the period of disability when a claim is in litigation.
D. Office workers often have an adversarial relationship with their employer that discourages a prompt return to work.

10. Which of the following would NOT be considered a "third party" in a workers compensation claim? 10.____

A. The manufacturer of a defective product that injured the worker.
B. The co-worker who accidentally injured the worker
C. A property owner (not the employer) who failed to properly maintain a safe workplace.
D. The owner of an animal that bit a worker.

11. Luther is on the steps of his employer's premises when he slips and sprains his ankle. He is taken to the employers' infirmary, where his ankle is iced down, and he is able to return to his desk for work within an hour. He is sore but feels fine otherwise. Which of the following is true? 11.____

A. The accident must be reported to the employer and the workers' compensation agency.
B. The accident must be reported to the employer and the workers' compensation agency only if it interferes with or affects Luther's ability to work.
C. The accident should only be reported if Luther was actively engaged in his job
D. Because Luther was not hospitalized and did not miss a significant amount of work, the accident does not need to be reported.

12. The following passage is from the California Labor Code: 12.____

*3501. (a) A child under the age of 18 years, or a child of any age found by any trier of fact, whether contractual, administrative, regulatory, or judicial, to be physically or mentally incapacitated from earning, shall be conclusively presumed to be wholly dependent for support upon a deceased employee-parent with whom that child is living at the time of injury resulting in death of the parent or for whose maintenance the parent was legally liable at the time of injury resulting in death of the parent, there being no surviving totally dependent parent.*
*(b) A spouse to whom a deceased employee is married at the lime of death shall be conclusively presumed to be wholly dependent for support upon the deceased employee if the surviving spouse earned thirty thousand dollars ($30,000) or less in the twelve months immediately preceding the death.*
John, a worker at a Los Angeles foundry, is killed in an accident. His wife, Imelda, is a teacher whose salary is $50,00(3 a year. John and Imelda have three children: Rose, 15 years old; Vincent, 13, and Jennifer, 10. John's son from a previous marriage, Brent, is 19 and lives in the same household.
Based on the above excerpt from the labor code, how many members of John's household could be considered "total dependents?"

A. 0
B. 1
C. 3
D. 4

13. A worker has an average weekly wage of $1000, which in her state qualifies her for a $600 weekly maximum disability benefit. As a result of a work-related accident, the worker's income was reduced to an average of $700 for several weeks after the accident. Under the workers' compensation plan, a weekly disability benefit is equal to the percentage of income lost as a result of sickness or accident multiplied by the maximum weekly disability benefit. In this case, the worker's average weekly benefit would be 13.____

A. $60
B. $180
C. $200
D. $300

14. In most jurisdictions, newer disability rating schedules allow physicians to rely on ______ the purpose of calculating a rating. 14.____

I. objective findings
II. subjective complaints by the employee, such as pain
III. work restrictions

A. I only
B. I and II
C. I and III
D. I, II and III

15. Disputes or disagreements over benefit entitlement can occur at any time in the life of a workers' compensation claim and can arise over any issue. Which of the following is LEAST likely to be one of these issues? 15.____

A. extent of permanent partial disability or entitlement to ongoing wage-loss benefits
B. whether the client is truly sick or injured
C. whether the current disability is related to the work-related injury or disease
D. entitlement to permanent total disability benefits and, if entitled, for how much and how long

16. The most common type of workers' compensation claim is caused by 16.____

A. a long-brewing situation that has reached a "breaking point"
B. a sudden and unexpected occurrence
C. a fairly long and unsuccessful treatment regimen
D. employee dissatisfaction

17. Which of the following is NOT an approach used to settle a workers' compensation claim? 17.____

A. Public hearing
B. Direct Settlement
C. Union arbitration
D. Agreement settlement

18. In California, a payment that has been unreasonably delayed or refused by an insurer is subject to a penalty of 25 percent or $10,000, whichever is less. 18.____

Herman does not get his disability check in the amount of $340 until four weeks past the date it is due. For this period, if the insurer's delay is found to be unreasonable, Herman's insurer owes him a total of

A. $85
B. $255
C. $340
D. $425

19. An employer who has been authorized by the appropriate agency to administer and pay directly on employee compensation claims is described as 19.____

A. self-insured
B. immune from action
C. in compliance
D. pre-qualified

20. Common reasons for an employee's challenge of an assigned disability rating include 20.____

I. wrong occupation or occupational group
II. wrong work restrictions given by physician
III. incomplete or inaccurate medical history used by the treating doctor
IV. age was not taken correctly into account

A. I and II
B. II and III
C. III and IV
D. I, II, III and IV

21. The ______ of some workers compensation programs is payable in the event of accidental death and, in some cases, accidental dismemberment. 21.____

A. total disability
B. flatline
C. whole life
D. principal sum

22. A visibly upset claimant asks an examiner to index her claim, even though the required medical forms have not yet been received at the department, because she desperately needs her benefit to be paid in order to pay for child care. The claimant assures the examiner that her physician has said she will qualify for a total temporary disability benefitand that the report can simply be slipped into the file after it is put into the system. Instead of directly saying "no" to the claimant, the examiner would MOST effectively begin her response by saying: 22.____

A. "Here's what we can do to get your claim moving through the system as quickly as possible."
B. "Even if your claim were filed, I couldn't simply hand you a check today."

C. "What is the worst that can happen to you if you don't pay for your child care this very day?"
D. "It would be against the law for me to do that."

23. Which of the following types of workers is MOST likely to be covered by a compulsory workers' compensation system? 23.____

A. office assistant
B. musician
C. farm worker
D. teacher

Questions 24 and 25 refer to Table A, below:

Table B
Number of paid claims (1,000s)

| Injury year | Indemnity claims | Medical-only claims | Total claims |
|---|---|---|---|
| 1984 | 40.2 | 103.2 | 143.4 |
| 1985 | 39.1 | 102.8 | 141.8 |
| 1988 | 37.8 | 101.2 | 138.7 |
| 1987 | 39.2 | 103.4 | 142.5 |
| 1988 | 42.0 | 109.9 | 151.9 |
| 1989 | 42.5 | 113.2 | 155.6 |
| 1990 | 42.6 | 113.3 | 155.8 |
| 1991 | 42.0 | 111.2 | 153.2 |
| 1992 | 39.4 | 112.8 | 152.2 |
| 1993 | 37.7 | 117.0 | 154.7 |
| 1994 | 37.1 | 125.4 | 162.5 |
| 1995 | 34.0 | 129.1 | 163.1 |
| 1996 | 33.8 | 131.4 | 165.2 |
| 1997 | 33.6 | 134.7 | 168.3 |
| 1998 | 32.8 | 134.4 | 167.2 |
| 1999 | 34.1 | 133.1 | 167.2 |
| 2000 | 34.7 | 132.5 | 167.1 |
| 2001 | 31.7 | 121.3 | 153.1 |
| 2002 | 29.4 | 109.1 | 138.6 |
| 2003 | 27.5 | 100.2 | 127.6 |
| 2004 | 26.5 | 97.4 | 124.0 |

24. The year in which the highest number of medical claims were filed was 24.____

A. 1984
B. 1990
C. 1997
D. 2000

25. The period during which total claims increased by the greatest number was 25.____

A. 1987-1988
B. 1991-1992
C. 1993-1994
D. 2001-2002

# KEY (CORRECT ANSWERS)

1. B
2. C
3. A
4. C
5. B
6. D
7. B
8. D
9. C
10. C
11. A
12. A
13. B
14. A
15. B
16. B
17. C
18. D
19. A
20. D
21. D
22. A
23. A
24. C
25. A

# TEST 3

DIRECTIONS: Each question or incomplete statement is followed by several suggested answers or completions. Select the one that BEST answers the question or completes the statement. *PRINT THE LETTER OF THE CORRECT ANSWER IN THE SPACE AT THE RIGHT.*

1. When the employer is classified by type, the ______ rating method is used to determine the premium rate. 1.____

   A. schedule
   B. manual
   C. retrospective
   D. experience

2. Janet Smith, an employee of Yardbirds, Inc., suffers an accident on the job that has left her with a permanent partial disability. Before the accident, Janet worked 40 hours a week at a job that paid $10.00 an hour. After the accident, Janet returned to lighter-duty job that paid $8.00 an hour, again for a 40-hour week. 2.____

   Using a factor of 4.333 to arrive at a monthly figure, calculate Janet Smith's loss in earning capacity.

   A. $231.09 per month
   B. $346.64
   C. $887.96
   D. $1386.56

3. Each of the following is a hazard associated with occupational disease, EXCEPT: 3.____

   A. sunlight
   B. noise
   C. exposure to toxic chemicals
   D. cigarette smoke

4. ______ lost-wages benefits are paid to workers' compensation claimants for non-medical loss resulting from an injury or illness. 4.____

   A. Subrogation
   B. Capitalization
   C. Valuation
   D. Indemnity

5. Common law requires that employers exercise reasonable care for the safety of their employees, including the specific duty to 5.____

   I. provide a safe work area and maintain the premises in safe condition
   II. warn employees of inherent dangers in the workplace, even those that are readily apparent
   III. provide enough competent employees for the work demanded
   IV. establish and enforce safety rules, in some cases to the point of discharging employees who repeatedly violate these rules

A. I and II
B. I, II and III
C. II, III and IV
D. I, II, III and IV

6. Which of the following is NOT a type of rating plan that is typically used to calculate workers' compensation premiums? 6.____

A. Experience rating
B. Manual rating
C. Assigned risk plans
D. Premium discount plan

Questions 7 and 8 refer to the information below:

A state workers compensation program has a rehabilitative employment program that works as follows: a worker who works in an approved rehabilitative employment program will receive a standard total disability benefit (75 percent of average weekly wage) reduced by 50 percent of the income received for each week of rehabilitative employment.

Mike Spacely has worked for his company for six years, and his annual salary was $40,000 when he became disabled. He received total disability benefits for 14 weeks and then began work in an approved rehabilitative employment program. Because of his disability, Mike can only work 4 hours a day, and now earns $ 140 a week in rehabilitative employment.

7. During his 14 weeks of total disability, Mike earned a weekly benefit of approximately 7.____

A. $507
B. $578
C. $647
D. $769

8. During his rehabilitative employment, Mike earned a combined total of about ______, in both benefits and salary. 8.____

A. $507
B. $578
C. $647
D. $769

9. In a ______ for workers' compensation, the only variable affecting the premium that should change between the inception of the policy and an audit is payroll. 9.____

A. retrospective rating
B. guaranteed cost
C. sliding scale dividend
D. retention

10. The workers' compensation system was derived from the principle of vicarious liability, a tort doctrine that imposes responsibility upon one person for the failure of another. Another term for vicarious liability is ______ liability. 10.____

A. imputed
B. displaced
C. disputed
D. contributory

11. Under the standard workers compensation policy, the insurer agrees to make certain payments in addition to the statutory benefits. These additional payments typically include each of the following, EXCEPT 11.____

A. litigation costs levied against the employer
B. payments required due to failure to comply with health and safety regulations
C. premiums for appeal bonds or bonds to release attachments
D. interest accruing on a judgement until the insurer offers the amount due under the policy

12. The final step in compiling a disability rating is usually to 12.____

A. adjust for the worker's occupational grouping
B. adjust for diminished future earning capacity
C. adjust for the worker's age on the date of injury
D. apply the impairment standard

13. Which of the following is a medical test in which a medical practitioner uses an instrument to measure the range of motion in a joint? 13.____

A. Joint calibration
B. Flexion test
C. Valsalva maneuver
D. Goniometry

14. To protect some state and private insurers, a(n) ______ policy allows a reinsurer to reimburse a portion of a workers compensation claim with payments to the insurer after the insurer has made payments for a specified number of months of total disability. 14.____

A. surplus-share
B. quota-share
C. excess-of-time
D. excess-of-loss

15. Survivors who are entitled to compensation on a death claim generally include certain classes of dependents, including 15.____

I. the surviving spouse
II. surviving minor children, including adopted children
III. a grandparent who was living with, and dependent on, the de cedent
IV. an uncle who was not described by the statute (i.e., lived apart from the decedent) but can prove his dependency on the decedent

A. I only
B. I and II
C. I, II and III
D. I, II, III and IV

16. About two-thirds of U.S. state workers' compensation systems use rate-making standards established by the 16.____

   A. National Council on Compensation Insurance (NCCI)
   B. National Workers Compensation Defense Network (NWCDN)
   C. National Institute for Occupational Safety and Health (NIOSH)
   D. Federal Occupational Safety and Health Administration (OSHA)

17. Gerda has worked as a commissioned sales representative for Robo-cash since February 1 of 2005. On August 6 of 2007, she is injured on the job. Gerda's wages depend on her sales and are different every week. To calculate Gerda's weekly wage for the purpose of a workers' compensation claim, one should 17.____

   A. list all her weekly wages from 2/1/2005 to 11/6/2007. Then take the wage earned during the lowest-paying week, add it to the wage earned during the highest-paying week, and divide by two
   B. take Gerda's total earnings from 2/1/2005 to 11/6/2007 and divide by the total number of weeks she worked.
   C. list all her weekly wages from 2/1/2005 to 11/6/2007. Then find the median by dropping, alternately, each of the highest- or lowest-paying weeks until only one wage remains. If it is an even-numbered period of weeks, add the last two remaining wages and divide by one.
   D. consider only wages earned during the previous year, taking Gerda's total earnings from 11/6//2006 to 11/6/ 2007, and dividing by the total number of weeks she worked

18. A fully covered dependent of a disabled worker is eligible for 50% of federal disability benefits if the dependent is ______ of age or younger. 18.____

   A. 18
   B. 19
   C. 21
   D. 24

19. An employee who files a job-related stress claim must typically present a case in which work stress can be proven to have caused ______ percent of the psychiatric disability. 19.____

   A. 33
   B. 51
   C. 76
   D. 100

20. Workers' compensation claims generally fall into three categories. Which of the following is NOT one of them? 20.____

   A. Occupational disease
   B. Discrimination
   C. Injury
   D. Death

21. Most federal and state laws regarding workplace violence uphold the view that 21.____

A. employers' measures to prevent workplace violence should follow OSHA guidelines
B. employers are fail to prevent or abate a recognized violence hazard in the workplace may be held liable under the general duty clause
C. violence is unpredictable and therefore difficult, if not impossible, to prevent
D. unless the employer personally committed the violence, he or she cannot be held liable

22. What part of a workers compensation insurance contract is illustrated below? 22.____
*(insurer) will pay for Total Disability or other covered loss resulting from Injuries or Sickness subject to the definitions, exclusions, and other provisions of this policy. Loss must begin while this policy is in force.*

A. benefit provision
B. general provisions
C. insuring clause
D. payment of claims provision

23. Which of the following is a term for the degree to which certain factors may have caused or contributed to a particular impairment or disability? 23.____

A. Assignation
B. Degree of causation
C. Aggravation
D. Apportionment

24. An employee may have a legitimate discrimination claim against an employer if she files or plans to file a workers' compensation claim and is 24.____
I. terminated from his or her job without good cause
II. given a notice of controversion
III. threatened with termination or other difficulties if she proceeds with the workers' compensation case
IV. demoted or given a cut in pay without a reasonable business necessi

A. I or II
B. I, III or IV
C. II and IV
D. I, II, III and IV

25. If a worker is partially disabled, the benefit is typically payable as follows: 25.____

$$\frac{A - B}{A} \text{ x monthly benefit for total disability}$$

where:
A = the worker's pre-claim monthly earnings
B = the worker's monthly earnings for work in which partial disability is claimed

Apply this formula to the following problem: John Doe had an annual salary of $66,000, and his employer's workers compensation insurance provided John a monthly total disability benefit of $3,500. After an on-the-job injury, John was able to return to work and earn $2,500 per month. His partial disability benefit would be

A. $546
B. $1,909
C. $2,154
D. $3500

# KEY (CORRECT ANSWERS)

1. D
2. B
3. D
4. D
5. D
6. C
7. B
8. C
9. B
10. A
11. B
12. C
13. D
14. D
15. C
16. A
17. B
18. A
19. B
20. B
21. B
22. C
23. D
24. B
25. B

# EXAMINATION SECTION
# TEST 1

DIRECTIONS: Each question or incomplete statement is followed by several suggested answers or completions. Select the one that BEST answers the question or completes the statement. *PRINT THE LETTER OF THE CORRECT ANSWER IN THE SPACE AT THE RIGHT.*

1. A presumption of work-relatedness exists if a worker 1.____

   A. is unable to work because of the disease
   B. can provide an opinion from a physician that the disease is work-related
   C. caught the disease from a co-worker
   D. contracts a scheduled disease while working in the specified occupation

2. Calculate the average weekly wage (AWW) of a ten-month (42-week) employee earning $30,000 annually. 2.____

   A. $576.92
   B. $714.29
   C. $989.56
   D. $1,260.00

3. Cosmetic surgery is MOST likely to be covered under workers' compensation if it is 3.____

   A. elective
   B. performed by an agency-approved surgeon
   C. used to correct a pre-existing condition
   D. required as a result of a workplace accident

4. The legal premise on which the workers' compensation system is based-workers give up the right to sue the employer in exchange for medical care of payment for their injuries-is known as 4.____

   A. conciliation
   B. sovereign immunity
   C. exclusive remedy
   D. covenants perpetual

5. When talking with a claimant about a workers' compensation claim, open questioning would NOT generally be useful for 5.____

   A. determining the claimant's needs
   B. confirming the completeness of a claim
   C. getting more information about a case
   D. defining a problem

6. The following passage is taken from the Workers' Compensation Provisions of the Consolidated Laws of New York State: 6.____

   *(b) The first payment of compensation shall become due on the fourteenth day of disability on which date or within four days thereafter all compensation then due shall be paid, and the compensation payable bi-weekly thereafter; but the board may determine that any payments may be made monthly or at any other period, as it may deem advisable.*

Ralph, covered under the state system, is injured on the job on February 15th. Which of the following compensation dates would NOT conform with the statute?

A. March 1
B. March 7
C. March 15
D. March 28

7. Which of the following factors is NOT used to calculate partial disability indemnity? 7.____

A. weekly or monthly indemnity amount
B. premium
C. loss of income
D. prior income

8. Which of the following is NOT a common-law legal defense available to employers who, in states where workers' compensation is elective, need to defend themselves against industrial accidents? 8.____

A. Assumption of risk
B. Comparative negligence
C. Contributory negligence
D. Master-servant rule (fellow employee negligence)

9. Of the following cases, the employee LEAST likely be eligible for workers' compensation would be one who 9.____

A. suffers panic attacks from hearing alarms or telephones ring loudly at work.
B. suffers neck strain, blurred vision, and headaches from working long shifts at a computer monitor
C. develops anxiety and panic attacks after witnessing a vicious assault and battery in the workplace
D. fractures a hip when slipping on the ice and falling on the paved entrance to the employer's front door

10. An examiner is discussing a workers' compensation case with a claimant whose injuries have left her severely disabled. The most appropriate way to communicate with this client would be to 10.____

A. watch for opportunities to offer assistance
B. use language that focuses on her as a person, rather than her disability
C. remember than disabled people are often uncomfortable or self-conscious when interacting with the nondisabled
D. ignore the disability entirely

11. Which of the following statements is TRUE? 11.____

A. While workers' compensation laws require employers to retain any punitive or exemplary damages assessed against them, employers' liability insurance provides coverage for punitive or exemplary damages.
B. Under most workers' compensation statutes, employers still retain contributory negligence as a defense to workers' compensation claims.

C. The maximum benefit payable under workers compensation typically equals or exceeds 66.67 percent of the state's average wages.
D. An employer is not responsible, under the legal principle *respondeat superior,* for an injury caused solely by the negligence of fellow employee.

12. Common loss control techniques used in workers compensation include 12.____
    I. loss reduction
    II. avoidance
    III. loss prevention
    IV. contractual transfer

A. I only
B. I and III
C. II, III and IV
D. I, II, III and IV

When a job-related injury results in a permanent disability, an employee may be entitled to permanent partial disability (PPD) benefits based upon the degree of permanent disability. Often a body part or "scheduled member" is functionally impaired, leading an examiner or adjuster to consult a list of scheduled body members and their respective value, in number of weeks. Questions and are based on the list below:

| | |
|---|---|
| Loss of thumb | 60 |
| Loss of first (index) finger | 35 |
| Loss of second finger | 30 |
| Loss of third finger | 25 |
| Loss of fourth finger | 20 |
| Loss of hand | 190 |
| Loss of arm | 250 |
| Loss of great toe | 40 |
| Loss of any other toe | 15 |
| Loss of foot | 150 |
| Loss of leg | 220 |
| Loss of eye | 140 |
| Loss of hearing in one ear | 50 |
| Loss of hearing in both ears | 175 |
| Permanent disfigurement, face or head | 150 |

This schedule represents the number of weeks of benefits payable for 100% loss, or loss of use, of the body member. If the permanent partial disability rating is less than 100%, the percentage rating is multiplied by the number of weeks shown.

13. A claimant has suffered what a physician has described as a 20 percent loss in the use of his thumb. This claimant would receive______ weeks of PPD benefits. 13.____

A. 6
B. 12
C. 48
D. 60

14. A factory employee has lost entire leg-a 100 percent loss-in a workplace accident. His PPD benefits would be paid 14.____

 A. indefinitely, since it is a total disability.
 B. for 147 weeks
 C. for 220 weeks.
 D. none, since it qualifies as a principal-sum loss.

15. The experience modifier designates the first $5,000 of any single loss in a workers' compensation claim to be the______ loss. 15.____

 A. instrumental
 B. primary
 C. intramarginal
 D. excess

16. Many states, such as New York, determine the compensation rate for temporary partial disability by calculating the average weekly wage, subtracting from that the current gross weekly wage being paid the injured employee, and multiplying that by two-thirds (.67). For example, if an employee were making $60(3 at an average weekly wage prior to the work injury and after the work injury was only making $400, the employee would be entitled to TPD benefits in the amount of______ per week 16.____

 A. $66
 B. $134
 C. $268
 D. $333

17. ______ plans provide workers' compensation insurance to companies that do not meet the underwriting criteria of private insurers. 17.____

 A. Assigned risk
 B. Monopolistic
 C. Competitive
 D. Prorated

18. In most workers' compensation hearings, the degree of proof necessary for a claimant to prevail is 18.____

 A. beyond reasonable doubt
 B. clear and convincing evidence
 C. absolute proof
 D. preponderance of evidence

19. Lisa has missed work off and on for several months because of poor health. After a series of tests and visits, Laura's doctor tells her she has toxins in her system because of exposure to cleaning chemicals at work. In her state, Lisa has one year from the "date of injury" to file a workers' compensation claim. For this purpose, the "date of injury" would be the day 19.____

 A. Lisa missed her first day of work
 B. Lisa made her first visit to the doctor
 C. Lisa's doctor told her that her injuries were work-related
 D. Lisa informed her employer of the doctor"s diagnosis

20. John was temporarily disabled for about a year. On reviewing his records, John finds that during that time, he was not paid the full temporary disability benefit he was due; instead of receiving the full amount due, $336, he was paid $250. In the state where John works, a payment that has been unreasonably delayed or refused by an insurer is subject to a penalty of 25 percent or $10,000, whichever is less. John is due a total amount of 20.____

A. $107.50
B. $172
C. $215
D. $375

21. Elliott, a corporate librarian, falls and injures his right knee at work. After his condition stabilizes, his doctor makes a finding of maximum medical improvement and gives him a "no heavy lifting" restriction. Elliott returns to his job at work, which does not involve heavy lifting. Typically, Elliott would 21.____

A. be eligible for a permanent disability benefit, because her inability to lift heavy objects would limit her ability to find work on the open job market.
B. not be eligible for either temporary or permanent disability benefits, since his job does not require heavy lifting.
C. be reassigned to lighter duty and paid a permanent disability benefit.
D. be eligible for a temporary disability benefit for the time he missed work, but no benefits thereafter, since his job doesn't involve heavy lifting.

22. Workers' compensation insurance rates are typically affected by each of the following factors, EXCEPT the 22.____

A. company's potential future losses
B. number of employees in the company
C. company's current profit or loss
D. types of work performed at the company

23. Which of the following terms is associated with third-party actions? 23.____

A. Conveyance
B. Subrogation
C. Mediation
D. Controversion

24. ______ is a legal principle stating that if a person voluntarily assumes a risk and is injured as a result, she cannot be indemnified for the losses. 24.____

A. Master-servant rule
B. Caveat emptor
C. Contributory negligence
D. Assumption of risk

25. While working for A-1 Cleaners, Mary inures her lower back on March 5, 2007. She files a workers' compensation claim and is treated by Dr. Jones, who treats her and sends her back to work with certain modifications and a 15 percent disability rating. Mary returns to work for A-I, and while still being treated for her previous injury, Mary suffers another back injury. She files another workers' compensation claim and is treated for that injury. Eventually Dr. Jones releases Mary back to work and writes a report stating that she reached maximum medical improvement on January 5, 2008 and has some permanent disability, caused half by the first injury and half by the second. The doctor gives Mary a restriction of "no heavy work." 25.____

The permanent disability settlement for a 15 percent rating is $8,040 under state law. The permanent disability settlement for a 30 percent rating is $21,420. According to the facts above, Mary is entitled to

A. no permanent disability benefits
B. one settlement of $8,040
C. two settlements of $8,040 each, for $ 16,080
D. one settlement of $21,420

---

# KEY (CORRECT ANSWERS)

1. D
2. B
3. D
4. C
5. B
6. B
7. B
8. B
9. A
10. B
11. C
12. D
13. B
14. C
15. B
16. B
17. A
18. D
19. C
20. C
21. A
22. C
23. B
24. D
25. D

---

# TEST 2

DIRECTIONS: Each question or incomplete statement is followed by several suggested answers or completions. Select the one that BEST answers the question or completes the statement. *PRINT THE LETTER OF THE CORRECT ANSWER IN THE SPACE AT THE RIGHT.*

1. Most workers' compensation statutes generally require 1.____

   A. immediate payment of lost wages compensation, but a waiting period before medical care benefits are paid
   B. immediate payment of both lost wages and medical care benefits
   C. a waiting period before lost wages compensation are payable, but immediate payment of medical care benefits
   D. a waiting period before payment of both lost wages and benefits

2. Generally, the type of accident or injury that is LEAST likely to be in dispute as a basis for a workers' compensation claim is one that happens 2.____

   A. during company-sanctioned travel time
   B. off-site
   C. during the lunch or coffee break
   D. at the place of employment

3. The greatest cause of employee death is 3.____

   A. machinery-related accidents
   B. falls
   C. vehicular accidents
   D. occupational diseases

4. In researching a claim's history, an examiner comes across the term "permanent and stationary" in an older medical record. As of about 2005, the meaning of this term was changed to the concept of 4.____

   A. maximum medical improvement
   B. permanent partial disability
   C. permanent total disability
   D. supplemental job displacement benefits

5. Which of the following cases is NOT an example of neutral risk? 5.____

   A. a teacher injured in a drive-by shooting that occurs as she is at work in her classroom
   B. an automobile mechanic who is bitten by a dog while emptying used oil into an outdoor receptacle
   C. a window-washer injured in a fall from a scaffold
   D. an sales assistant struck by a falling tree as she walked to her car to embark on a call

6. Harriet, landscape gardener, injures her knees from constantly kneeling at work. Her doctor reports that she has attained maximum medical improvement on March 1, with a 15 percent permanent disability, payable at $230 a week. Her employer did not offer her any type of modified alternative work by May 1, so her payments increased by 15 percent. Her ongoing permanent disability benefit is 6.____

   A. $245
   B. $264.50
   C. $299
   D. $460

7. Minimal conditions must be met before financial responsibility can be assigned to a claim for workers' compensation. Which of the following is NOT one of them? 7.____

   A. A work-related accident or disability covered by workers' compensation law occurred.
   B. The employee or claimant notified the employer of the accident or disability within the required time limit.
   C. The employer is found to have at least some liability for the accident or disability.
   D. A causal relationship exists between the accident and a resulting injury or disability.

8. The purpose of a probationary period is to 8.____

   A. eliminate the need for a Medical Examiner's report
   B. protect the insurer against material misrepresentation
   C. protect the insurer company against preexisting conditions
   D. protect the worker against adverse selection

9. Often, state boards can overturn a workers' compensation award granted by an administrative law judge. In such cases, the ruling is said to have been 9.____

   I. annulled
   II. rescinded
   III. controverted
   IV. voided

   A. I or II
   B. I, II or IV
   C. II, III or IV
   D. I, II, III or IV

10. Jason, a long-haul truck driver who lives in Grass Valley, California, is hired at a Sacramento branch office of Cosmic Freight, Inc., a company headquartered in Reno, Nevada. In the course of his employment, Jason is injured in an accident in Oregon. 10.____

    Which of the following would typically be TRUE?

    A. Jason must receive benefits from the California state system.
    B. Jason may receive benefits from both the California and Nevada workers compensation systems, but not from Oregon.
    C. Jason may select the most generous benefits from the three systems, but may not receive duplicate benefits.
    D. Jason must file his claim in Oregon, where the accident occurred.

11. Typically, modified or alternative work offered by an employer must pay at least______ percent of what the employee was paid at the time of his or her injury. 11.____

A. 34
B. 51
C. 85
D. 100

12. The______ benefit of some group insurance funds waives any premiums that fall due after the insured has been totally disabled for a specified period. 12.____

A. total disability
B. accelerated
C. waiver of premium
D. minimum participation

13. Workers' compensation statutes generally cover most______ employments, whether they are hazardous or not. 13.____

I. public
II. private
III. domestic
IV. agricultural

A. I and II
B. I, II and III
C. II and III
D. I, II, III and IV

14. The time between the first day of disability and the day to which the disability must continue before it can result in the insured receiving benefits is known as the waiting or______ period 14.____

A. probationary
B. eligibility
C. elimination
D. grace

15. Which of the following is the term for a deviation from normal in a body part or organ system and its functioning? 15.____

A. Impairment
B. Physical restriction
C. Disability
D. Handicap

16. Under federal OSHA regulations, all employers with______ or more employees must maintain records of, and report, occupational injuries and occupational illnesses. 16.____

A. 8
B. 11
C. 30
D. 100

17. Which of the following is a premium adjustment used for employers who are too small to qualify for an experience modifier? 17.____

A. Merit rating
B. Manual rating
C. Attenuator
D. Step-down

18. John Wilson works for Universal Construction, LLC. One day, while operating a backhoe, Wilson ruptured a water line, causing a flood that damaged several nearby buildings. While attempting to flee the rising waters, Wilson fractured his ankle. Most likely, 18.____

A. Wilson is liable for the damages he caused, and is entitled to workers' compensation, if he is found to have deliberately ruptured the water line.
B. Universal and Wilson will be jointly liable for damage to the building, but Wilson will be eligible for workers' compensation, whether he deliberately ruptured the water line or not.
C. If he deliberately ruptured the water line, Wilson is liable for the damage he caused and is not entitled to workers' compensation.
D. Whether Wilson meant to rupture the water line or not, his negligence in operating the backhoe will disqualify him from receiving workers' compensation.

19. Several U.S. states, along with Puerto Rico and the U.S. Virgin Islands, require all workers compensation insurance to be placed with the state or territorial fund. This approach is known as the______. state fund 19.____

A. competitive
B. monopolistic
C. autocratic
D. assigned risk

20. In determining a disability rating, a rater will include the______ ______, which is a whole-person impairment rating under the AMA Guides. 20.____

A. impairment number
B. impairment standard
C. schedule amount
D. impairment variant

21. On a telephone call with an employee who is awaiting a decision on an indexed claim, an examiner explains to the caller that even if he knew anything about the claim's progress through the process, he could not reveal anything about the progress of the claim. In order to best serve this customer, the examiner's response to him would be LEAST helpful if it involved 21.____

A. explaining to the customer why no information is available yet
B. quoting the passage in the state laws or regulations that prohibited this kind of communication
C. make specific statements regarding what can be revealed about the claims process
D. offering alternative solutions to the customer

22. Typically, a rated premium is based on dollars per $______ of an employer's payroll. 22.____

A. 10
B. 100
C. 1,000
D. 10,000

23. Joe, who has worked for seven years at Geraldo's Auto Body, receives a substantial raise in July. In September, he slips on some grease on the shop floor and falls, fracturing his pelvis. In most jurisdiction's, Joe's average weekly wage will represent 23.____

A. his average weekly earnings over the last 52 weeks
B. his average weekly earnings up to July
C. his weekly wage at the time of his injury
D. the average between his current wage and the wage he was paid before his July raise

24. Pete, a firefighter, injures his back fighting a fire, and on August 15, his doctor submits a report of maximum medical improvement with a 15 percent disability rating, which is payable at $230 a week. On September 10, Pete's employer offers him an office job that will not require field work, and Paul accepts. His payments decrease by 15 percent, and his ongoing permanent disability payments are 24.____

A. $0 24.____
B. $195.50
C. $245
D. $264.50

25. If a worker is partially disabled, the benefit is typically payable as follows: 25.____

$\frac{A-B}{A}$ x weekly benefit for total disability A

where:
A= the worker's pre-claim weekly earnings

B= the worker's weekly earnings for work in which partial disability is claimed

Apply this formula to the following problem: Stan Adams earns an average of $700 a week at Oil Changers, under a workers' compensation system that pays him a maximum weekly benefit of 75 percent of his average weekly wage. After slipping on some oil at work and wrenching his back, Stan is unable to change the oil in automobiles on the lift. His supervisor moves him to the position of greeter, where he writes down orders for incoming customers. The job pays only 80 percent of what Stan was earning as an oil changer, and he qualifies for partial disability.
What is Stan's weekly partial disability benefit?

A. $112
B. $140
C. $200
D. $560

# KEY (CORRECT ANSWERS)

1. C
2. D
3. C
4. A
5. C
6. B
7. C
8. C
9. B
10. C
11. C
12. C
13. A
14. C
15. A
16. B
17. A
18. C
19. B
20. B
21. B
22. B
23. C
24. B
25. A

# TEST 3

DIRECTIONS: Each question or incomplete statement is followed by several suggested answers or completions. Select the one that BEST answers the question or completes the statement. *PRINT THE LETTER OF THE CORRECT ANSWER IN THE SPACE AT THE RIGHT.*

1. A_______ fund is typically a state agency that reimburses self-insuring companies or insurance carriers for part of the workers' compensation costs in certain instances when an employee with a pre-existing permanent partial disability is injured on the job. 1.____

   A. group insurance
   B. retrospective
   C. second injury
   D. reinsurance

2. The two types of workers' compensation laws are 2.____

   A. statutory and administrative
   B. state-fund and self-insured
   C. criminal and civil
   D. compulsory and elective

3. The temporary total disability benefit is available to an employee when the employee is completely unable to work for a period of time. In a certain state, the TTD benefit is determined by multiplying the average weekly wage by two-thirds, or .67. As of the last regulatory revision, the maximum TTD benefit rate is $615.00. The minimum benefit rate is $104.00. 3.____

   Jack, who earns $600 a week, is injured on the job and is unable to work for a period of several weeks. His weekly benefit during that period would be

   A. 104
   B. 400
   C. 600
   D. 615

4. Each of the following is considered an accident prevention strategy, EXCEPT 4.____

   A. safety training and communications
   B. protective equipment
   C. selective hiring and firing
   D. work teams

5. Claims that are accepted by the employer or the insurer, but which may have unresolved issues, are typically sent by a state board or department to a process known as 5.____

   A. vetting
   B. conciliation
   C. arbitration
   D. controversion

6. For which of the following cases would the establishment of a valid workers' compensation claim be MOST difficult? 6.____

   A. A data-entry clerk who suffers tendonitis due to repetitive stress while telecommuting from his home computer
   B. A woman who slips and breaks her pelvis in the company lunchroom
   C. An office assistant who was attending an off-site business luncheon
   D. A traveling salesperson who is involved in an automobile accident while he is making his weekly rounds

7. Calculate the average weekly wage (AWW) of a 196-day employee earning $30,000. 7.____

   A. $576.92
   B. $714.29
   C. $765.30
   D. $1,071.43

8. The federal continual-training requirement states that employers must provide safety training for all new hires and those transferred into a department, 8.____

   A. even if only for one day
   B. if for a continuous period of five days
   C. if for a continuous period of 30 days
   D. when the transfer is meant to be permanent

9. The main reason an employer would protest a decision on a workers' compensation claim is because the employer feels that the claim 9.____

   A. does not adequately compensate the worker and his or her family
   B. results in a benefit that is greater than the claimant's base pay
   C. is fraudulent
   D. may effect its experience rating and result in a higher premium

10. The______ doctrine states that employees who are injured on the job are entitled to workers' compensation benefits, but they cannot sue their employers for additional amounts. 10.____

   A. Feres
   B. quasi-contract
   C. generalized immunity
   D. exclusive remedy

11. Which of the following form titles would be filed by an insurance carrier or approved self-insurer? 11.____

   A. Application for Re-opening of Claim
   B. Notice that Right to Compensation is Controverted
   C. Application for Approval of Non-Schedule Adjustment
   D. Claim for Compensation and Notice of Commencement of Third Party Action

12. When a workers' compensation claim is caused by an occupational disease, most statutes establish a time limit for notifying one"s employer of either______ from the date of disablement, or from the date when the claimant knew or should have known that the disease was due to the nature of the employment. 12.____

A. 3 or 6 months
B. 1 or 2 years
C. 3 or 5 years
D. 5 or 10 years

13. Workers' compensation insurers, whether state or private, play an important role in loss control. They often assist employers by offering 13.____
I. financial incentives
II. double indemnity protections
III. risk management information services
IV. accident prevention services

A. I, II and III
B. I, III and IV
C. II and IV
D. I, II, III and IV

14. A claimant has telephoned the examiner and appears to be mildly irritated to learn that all the required forms have not been submitted in order for his claim to be indexed. The most appropriate action for the examiner to take in order to attempt a resolution of this situation would be to 14.____

A. demonstrate a calm, emotional neutrality
B. allow the customer some time to vent her frustration
C. enlist the claimant's help in generating solutions
D. quietly but firmly suggest that the claimant calm down

15. When a workplace accident occurs, the employer can sustain a variety of losses that are not covered by its workers compensation or employers liability insurance. These uninsured losses typically include each of the following, EXCEPT costs or expenses that are 15.____

A. incurred by the insured at the insurer"s request
B. incurred because of missed deadlines or overtime expenses resulting from the loss of the employee
C. associated with damage to machines, tools, or other property affected by the accident
D. associated with hiring and training a new employee for the vacant position

16. In the state where Joshua works, employees are entitled to workers' compensation benefits up to two-thirds of their average weekly wage, within the minimum and maximum amounts allowed by law. Joshua is injured at work on February, 2007, and is assigned a 12 percent disability rating. The maximum average weekly amount allowed for an injury occurring in 2007 is $180 for a partial disability rating under 15 percent; $220 for a PD rating from 15 to 24.75 percent; $250 for a PD rating from 25 to 69.75 percent; and $280 for a PD rating of 70 percent or higher. Joshua, whose average weekly wage is $210 a week, is entitled to a maximum benefit amount of 16.____

A. $140
B. $180
C. $210
D. $220

17. The category of risk that is generally most problematic in determining the compensability of a work injury is______ risk. 17.____

A. directly employment-related
B. neutral
C. financial
D. personal

18. Most disability rating schedules use______ as the median age for adjusting a rating. 18.____

A. 32
B. 39
C. 45
D. 50

19. The partial disability benefit 19.____

A. forces the worker to remain at home until he or she fully recovers.
B. is payable for only a fraction of the policy's total disability benefit period.
C. encourages injured employees to return to work.
D. pays the insured for a presumptive disability.

20. The term for any single claim that exceeds $5,000 is classified by the experience modifier as a(n)______ loss. 20.____

A. excess
B. proterm
C. nonstandard
D. rated

21. In California, no temporary disability benefits are paid for the first three days off work, unless the injury requires hospital ization or the employee misses more than 14 days of work. Frank is injured at work and takes 11 days off to recover. He was not hospitalized. He is entitled to______ days of temporary disability. 21.____

A. 3
B. 8
C. 11
D. 14

22. An employee covered by workers' compensation is usually 22.____

A. required to work with an insurer- or state-approved physician for workers' compensation puiposes, without condition
B. required to work with an insurer- or state-approved physician for workers' compensation purposes, provided the insurer or state agency names the physician before an injury or accident occurs
C. allowed to choose her treating physician for workers' compensation purposes, without condition
D. allowed to choose her treating physician for workers' compensation purposes, provided the employer is notified of the employee's choice before the injury or accident occurs

23. The following passage is from the California Labor Code: 23.____
*3302. (a) (l) When a licensed contractor enters an agreement with a temporary employment agency, employment referral service, labor contractor, or other similar entity for the entity to supply the contractor with an individual to perform acts or contracts for which the contractor's license is required under Chapter 9 (commencing with Section 7000) of Division 3 of the Business and Professions Code and the licensed contractor is responsible for supervising the employee's work, the temporary employment agency, employment referral service, labor contractor, or other similar entity shall pay workers' compensation premiums based on the contractor's experience modification rating.*
Julius Jones, an office worker, is a client of People Power, Inc., a temporary employment agency. ABC Corporation, a large construction contractor, is hiring clerical staff for a large upcoming project in the downtown area: a new federal government office building complex. ABC hires Julius Jones, as a client of People Power, to perform clerical duties during the project.
According to the section of the Labor Code above, the premiums for Julius Jones's workers' compensation insurance are to be paid by

A. Julius Jones
B. ABC Corporation
C. People Power, Inc.
D. the federal government

24. Although workers' compensation is established as a "no-fault" system, this has proven to be no longer true, in certain cases, for______ injuries. 24.____

A. continuous trauma
B. psychiatric
C. disfiguring
D. respiratory

25. 25.____

**Table D**
**Types of Injury in which at least 10 Percent of Claims Reach Statutory MMI**

| | MMI Prior to104 Weeks | | MMI at 104 Weeks or More | |
|---|---|---|---|---|
| Body Part Injured | Number of Claims | Percent of Claims | Number of Claims | Percent of Claims |
| Head (unspecified) | 95 | 85.6% | 16 | 14.4% |
| Brain | 200 | 88.1% | 27 | 11.9% |
| Circulatory System | 104 | 86.7% | 16 | 13.3% |
| Muscle-skeletal System | 175 | 89.7% | 20 | 10.3% |
| Nervous System | 346 | 85.0% | 61 | 15.0% |
| Respiratory System | 131 | 85.1% | 23 | 14.9% |
| Nature of injury | | | | |
| Concussion | 199 | 88.0% | 27 | 12.0% |
| Cerebrovascular | 56 | 83.6% | 11 | 16.4% |
| Mental Disease | 134 | 80.7% | 32 | 19.3% |
| Ill-Defined Conditions | 393 | 86.4% | 62 | 13.6% |

Based on the data in Table D above, what type of injury or illness is most likely to result in a finding of maximum medical improvement after 104 weeks have passed?
A. Mental disease
B. Brain or Concussion
C. Musculo-skeletal
D. Ill-defined conditions

---

# KEY (CORRECT ANSWERS)

1. C
2. D
3. B
4. C
5. B
6. C
7. D
8. A
9. D
10. D
11. B
12. B
13. B
14. C
15. A
16. A
17. B
18. B
19. B
20. A
21. B
22. D
23. C
24. B
25. A

---

# Memory for Facts and Information

## EXAMINATION SECTION
## TEST 1

DIRECTIONS: The following questions test your ability to remember key facts and details. You are given a reading passage, which you will have approximately ten minutes to read. The reading selection should then be turned over. Then immediately answer the questions that refer to each passage. There will be between 9 and 17 questions for each passage. Please do NOT refer back to the reading passage at any time while you are answering the questions. Select the letter that represents the BEST of the four possible choices.

**The Mysterious Injury**

The Claim Resolution Board of the State Department of Labor and Industry has just issued its ruling after conducting a hearing to determine whether a claimant, Lisa Lindley, suffered a compensable injury arising out of and in the course of her employment on April 4th of the previous year. The claim includes medical and hospital benefits associated with the injury, as well as attorney's fees and pursuant costs.

Below are the Findings of Fact included in the hearing report.

*Findings of Fact:*

*1. The exhibits are admitted into evidence. Notice is taken of all forms filed with the Department in this matter.*

*2. The claimant has been employed with the defendant, GORTECH, as a team technician since August 24, 2000. Specifically, on April 4th of______, during the first shift (7:00 a.m. - 3:00 p.m.), the claimant was working on the Toyota assembly line.*

*3. Claimant claimed that while she was working on April 4, she injured her right knee when she tripped over a box of levers with her left leg and subsequently twisted her right knee. She described her injury as a "throbbing" sensation throughout her right knee. Moreover, as a manifestation of her injury, she claims her shin had red marks and the skin was broken.*

*4. Claimant further testified that she immediately informed the "lead team technician," Yolanda Tucker, of her injury. She stated that she could not recall Yolanda Tucker's response to claimant's reported injury. However, claimant contends that she approached Yolanda Tucker on numerous occasions between April 4 and April 16 to request the completion of an accident report. In her testimony, she claimed that Yolanda Tucker failed to complete an accident report on the incident until April 16.*

*5. After the completion of her work day, the claimant stated that she picked her son up at day care and took him home. Mr. Lindley testified that he recalled the claimant arrived home on a Friday limping and favoring her right leg. However, he was unable to verify whether the date the claimant injured herself was even within the month of April.*

*6. Mr. Lindley, in describing the claimant's injury, also testified that claimant limped in such a manner as to have been noticeable to individuals who worked with the claimant on the day of the alleged injury. However, of the eighteen (18) individuals who worked on the same line as the claimant on the date of the incident, none were capable of validating or confirming the claimant's injury.*

*7. On April 5, despite the claimant's complaints of knee pain, she worked a voluntary shift the day following the accident. Although claimant asserts that she worked on the 5th because she feared negative repercussions, such an assertion is contrary to her prior testimony wherein she stated that she reported her injury to Yolanda Tucker on April 4th. If the claimant had previously reported her work-related injury, she could not have rationally feared suffering a penalty for failing to work a voluntary shift the following day.*

*8. Yolanda Tucker has been employed by GORTECH for approximately six (6) years. Ms. Tucker works as a "lead team technician," supervising and monitoring the workers on her assigned line. In addition, Ms. Tucker has been trained as a "first responder," providing basic first aid to injured employees. During her testimony, Ms. Tucker denies receiving any report of the claimant's injury on April 4. In fact, Ms. Tucker testified that she was first made aware of the injury on April 16, when the claimant approached her and said: "Remember when I hurt my knee hist week and I told you about it?" In addition, having received first aid training, Ms. Tucker stated that if she had been made aware of the claimant's accident on April 4, she would have immediately treated her injury.*

*9. Ms. Tucker further stated that on April 16, when the claimant first reported her injury, she directed the claimant to Karen Stark, the company nurse, whose primary responsibility is managing worker's compensation injuries for GORTECH. Accordingly, on April 16, the claimant went to see Karen Stark.*

*10. Karen Stark testified that she directed the claimant to a supervisor in order for an accident report to be completed.*

*11. The claimant eventually completed an accident report (Defendant's Exhibit 2,). However, she was unable to state with certainty when she completed the report. Moreover, although she was initially unable to identify where she obtained the accident report form, she later recalled that she acquired it from the cafeteria. The claimant testified that she could not remember to whom she delivered the finished report nor could she recall if she had any conversations with this individual about the accident report when she turned it in.*

*12. The accident report completed by the claimant states that the accident occurred on April 7, instead of April 4. The claimant explained that she inserted the April 7th date into the report because a co-worker told her she injured herself on April 7th. However, the claimant could not identify the co-worker who told her that date.*

*13. Yolanda Tucker also filled out an accident report relative to this incident (Defendant's Exhibit 1). The date on this report was changed by the claimant from April 7th to April 4th. Yolanda Tucker testified that the claimant changed the date after it was revealed to her that the boxes which she allegedly tripped over were removed prior to April 7$^{th}$ and, therefore, she could not have been injured on that date.*

*14. With regards to the claimant's medical treatment for the injuries sustained in this incident, claimant first sought treatment from Mansour Naim, a licensed physicians' assistant at Orthopedic and Hand Surgery in Farmington, on April 17, almost two weeks after the accident.*

*15. The claimant has presented evidence of her fee agreement with her attorney for a contingency fee. She has also introduced evidence that her attorney has spent 33 hours in preparation of this case. Furthermore, she has submitted evidence of expenses in the amount of $97.65.*

1. The injury claimed by Lisa Lindley was to her 1.____

   A. left shin
   B. right foot
   C. left knee
   D. right knee

2. In his testimony, how sure of the date of Lisa Lindley's injury is her husband, Greg Lindley? 2.____

   A. Pretty sure
   B. Not sure at all
   C. Completely unaware of an injury
   D. Very sure

3. The reason given by the claimant, Lisa Lindley, for why she worked a voluntary shift on the day after her injury was that she 3.____

   A. feared "negative repercussions"
   B. felt much better
   C. was not actually injured until April 7$^{th}$
   D. did not want to leave her team shorthanded

4. Mrs. Lindley's claim of injury was validated by ______ of her co-workers. 4.____

   A. none
   B. 1
   C. 5
   D. 18

5. Who is Karen Stark? 5.____

   A. a licensed physicians' assistant at Orthopedic and Hand Surgery in Farmington
   B. a lead team technician at GORTECH
   C. the GORTECH company nurse
   D. a team technician who worked on the same line as Lisa Lindley

6. Yolanda Tucker testified that she was first made aware of the injury on 6.____

   A. April 4$^{th}$
   B. April 5$^{th}$
   C. April 16$^{th}$
   D. April 17$^{th}$

7. Regarding its effect on Lisa Lindley's case, her husband's testimony that she had a noticeable limp on the day of the accident appeared to 7.____

A. support her case, because she did not claim to have a noticeable limp
B. support her case, because the limp was not noticeable to anyone else who saw her that day
C. weaken her case, because he proved to be a credible witness with a good memory for facts
D. weaken her case, because the limp was substantiated by the company nurse

8. The claimant, Lisa Lindley, is able to state with certainty 8.____

A. how Yolanda Tucker responded to her claim of injury
B. where she obtained her accident report
C. when she completed her accident report
D. none of the above

9. Lisa Lindley's own accident report form was filed on 9.____

A. April $7^{th}$
B. April $16^{th}$
C. April $17^{th}$
D. it is unclear from the information in the passage when Ms. Lindley filed her report

10. Yolanda Tucker's job involves 10.____

I. supervising and managing employees
II. giving first aid to injured workers
III. managing worker's compensation injuries

A. I only
B. I and II
C. II and III
D. III only

11. The passage states that the claimant, Lisa Lindley, first sought medical treatment on April 11.____

A. $4^{th}$
B. $7^{th}$
C. $16^{th}$
D. $17^{th}$

12. Lisa Lindley's own explanation for why she changed the date of the accident on her report from April 4th to April 7th was that 12.____

A. a co-worker had told her that was when she injured herself
B. she had worked a voluntary shift on April 5th
C. her husband reminded her that was when she had come home limping
D. Yolanda Tucker reminded her that the boxes she tripped over were removed before April 7th

13. The passage states as an established fact that Lisa Lindley 13.____

    A. first sought medical treatment almost two weeks after her injury
    B. walked with a noticeable limp on April 4th
    C. lied about her reasons for working a voluntary shift on April 5th
    D. was not injured on April 4th

14. Lisa Lindley ultimately claimed that she obtained her accident report form from 14.____

    A. Yolanda Tucker
    B. the cafeteria
    C. Karen Stark
    D. Mansour Naim

15. The alleged cause of this accident was that Lisa Lindley 15.____

    A. hit her knee on a lever
    B. worked a voluntary shift the day after twisting her knee
    C. tripped over a box of levers
    D. dropped a lever on her knee

**Hiring Discrimination?**

The following is the text of a sworn affidavit filed by Martha J. Swinton, a social worker at Children's Agency, an outpatient psychiatric clinic. Ms. Swinton's affidavit was subpoenaed by an attorney for Cheryl Banks, a social worker who has filed a lawsuit against Children's Agency, alleging hiring discrimination.

AFFIDAVIT OF MARTHA J. SWINTON
Your affiant, MARTHA J. SWINTON, being duly sworn, deposes and states:

I am a social work practitioner at Children's Agency, an outpatient psychiatric clinic run by the King County Social Services, and have been so employed for five years. Last year, I completed my Master of Social Work degree at Coe University, having practiced social work for several years with an undergraduate degree. The Director of Social Services at the Children's Agency, Elsa Lang, is my supervisor. We use a team model in our work, with any particular team consisting of at least a social worker, a psychologist, and a psychiatrist. Sometimes other professionals, such as educational specialists, early childhood development specialists, and social group workers are also on the teams. I have first-rate colleagues in whom I can confide about clinical and ethical issues. Continuous learning is valued, especially as it relates to clinical practice.

Last year, while I was employed by Children's Agency, Cheryl Banks applied to the agency for a job as a social worker. Six years earlier, I had seen Cheryl as a client while working for an emergency service at Adult Hospital, a psychiatric facility for adults.

My contact with Cheryl at Adult Hospital was brief. She came to be admitted to the hospital as her psychiatric condition was deteriorating. Cheryl told me she was a social worker with a Master's degree in Social Work (MSW) and had been in and out of psychiatric hospitals for many years. I located her chart, noted that she was previously diagnosed with schizophrenia, undifferentiated type, and did the basic paperwork that social workers do on admission. I consulted with the admitting psychiatrist, and took her to the hospital ward. It was a simple, routine admission; there were no police or court documents, and she was a voluntary client.

At the time I had conversations with several of the other workers at Adult Hospital, and I recall that I found the situation unsettling. These feelings had to do with the fact that I-to my mind, a young and inexperienced social worker, who would soon be leaving my position to pursue an MSW—was admitting an older and more experienced professional with an MSW to a psychiatric hospital. I was later able to put the event in perspective—having an academic degree, after all, had never meant that one could not have a mental illness.

So now, several years later, when I had my own MSW, Cheryl came for a job interview at Children's Agency, where I was employed. I had no responsibility for employment decisions-personnel matters were handled by Elsa Lang, my supervisor, who was the Director of Social Services, and Dr. Michael Conroy, the psychiatrist, who was also the Executive Director. While I had no input in personnel decisions, I considered myself to be in an ethical dilemma.

On the one hand, I was concerned about whether Cheryl would function as a competent professional colleague. I had no idea whether her illness was in remission, or whether it might have an impact on clients or her co-workers—including myself.

On the other hand, my knowledge of her illness was unquestionably confidential. And I felt that I had no right to suggest that a person with a mental illness should not be hired, or to divulge information about her condition—which I must necessarily assume to have been in the past—to anyone.

In the end, I made the painful decision not to mention Cheryl's condition to anyone at Children's Agency. When I learned five weeks later that Elsa and Dr. Conroy had decided to hire another social worker, Solomon Ross, I asked why they had chosen him. Ms. Lang replied that after interviewing all the finalists—a group that included Cheryl Banks—she and Dr. Conroy had felt that, besides being the most qualified candidate in terms of his education and work experience, he was also the candidate with the most dynamic and likeable personality.

16. According to the passage, Children's Agency offers 16.____

A. psychiatric care
B. foster care placements
C. child protective services
D. needy family benefits

17. Martha Swinton describes the working climate at Children's Agency as 17.____

A. light and whimsical
B. open and collegial
C. rigid and hierarchical
D. authoritarian and fear-driven

18. Martha Swinton has worked at Children's Agency for 18.____

A. 2 years B. 3 years C. 5 years D. 6 years

19. In the affidavit, Martha Swinton recalls that Cheryl Bank's admission to Adult Hospital made her feel 19.____

A. judgmental B. angry C. sad D. uncomfortable

20. When Martha Swinton was working at Adult Hospital, Cheryl Banks entered the facility 20.____

A. on her own initiative
B. as part of a court order
C. in restraints
D. and caused quite a disturbance

21. Who is the Director of Social Services at Children's Agency? 21.____

A. Michael Conroy B. Elsa Lang
C. Martha Swinton D. Solomon Ross

22. Martha Swinton's role in hiring decisions at Children's Agency can best be described as 22.____

A. strictly advisory
B. serving only a pre-screening function
C. focused on the agency's compliance with hiring regulations
D. Martha Swinton has no role at all in hiring decisions

23. There is evidence contained in Martha Swinton's affidavit that Children's Agency gave Cheryl Banks' candidacy for the position some serious consideration. The strongest evidence is probably the fact that 23.____

A. Martha Swinton told nobody of Cheryl Banks' mental illness
B. Cheryl Banks was a finalist for the position.
C. Solomon Ross was found to be not only more qualified, but more likeable
D. Cheryl Banks was forthright and proactive in disclosing her past mental illness

24. The content of this affidavit makes it seem most likely that Cheryl Banks believes she was not hired because the people responsible for personnel decisions at Children's Agency 24.____

A. thought she had a bad personality
B. had been listening to Martha Swinton's lies about her
C. found an applicant with better credentials
D. were aware of her mental illness and feared it would interfere with her work

25. When Solomon Ross was hired by Children's Agency, Martha Swinton felt 25.____

A. vindicated
B. sorry for Cheryl Banks
C. relieved
D. It isn' t possible from the text of the affidavit to tell how Martha Swinton felt about the hiring of Solomon Ross

# KEY (CORRECT ANSWERS)

1. D
2. B
3. A
4. A
5. C
6. C
7. B
8. D
9. D
10. B
11. D
12. A
13. A
14. B
15. C
16. A
17. B
18. C
19. D
20. A
21. B
22. D
23. B
24. D
25. D

# TEST 2

DIRECTIONS: The following questions test your ability to remember key facts and details. You are given a reading passage, which you will have approximately ten minutes to read. The reading selection should then be turned over. Then immediately answer the questions that refer to each passage. There will be between 9 and 17 questions for each passage. Please do NOT refer back to the reading passage at any time while you are answering the questions. Select the letter that represents the BEST of the four possible choices.

**Diablo Publishing**

Garrett Longo is a civil rights investigator for the state Department of Law who is investigating a claim of sexual harassment at Diablo Publishing, a large custom publisher. The lawyer for Vivian Vance, the plaintiff in the case, has submitted the following brief to Garrett Longo:

VANCE V. DIABLO PUBLISHING

*I. Background. Diablo Publishing, Inc. ( "Diablo") is the publisher of numerous custom magazines highlighting the achievements and programs of many businesses and agencies throughout the region. Some of its best-known publications include The Year in Public Health and The Official Starco Magazine, a monthly publication produced for a large regional chain of retail department stores. Gray Minot is the Executive Vice President in charge of Diablo's marketing, and is largely perceived by his peers–and especially by the company's founder and Chief Executive Officer, Mathilda Ward–to have been responsible for Diablo's substantial increase in revenue over the past two years.*

*Vivian Vance is a 26-year-old graphics and layout editor who was recently hired to bring a more modern, updated look to Diablo's publications. Both Minot and Vance work in Diablo's downtown main office, in offices that are nearly across the hall from each other. Vance reports to John Stamps, Diablo's Editor-in-Chief. Stamps is a friend of Gray Minot's, and was also a member of the same fraternity when the two were in college together.*

*II. The Policy. The last time Diablo revised and reissued its employment policy was two years ago, in the year 20___. The manual, which is about 40 pages long, contains the following Equal Employment Opportunity policy statement:*

> *Diablo is committed to maintaining a discrimination-free workplace, based on equal opportunity for all. Harassment, especially sexual harassment, should be reported at once to the appropriate manager or executive.*

*A copy of the manual was distributed to each department head, including Minot.*

*II. The Facts. Minot's success over the past two years has been attributed to his ability to inspire a team atmosphere among the sales staff. Minot has fostered this atmosphere by hosting monthly outings for the marketing staff at a local restaurant and tavern, the Elephant Bar. These outings typically involve drinking, dancing, and sometimes a "surprise" event; one of the most memorable surprises in recent memory was an exotic dancer jumping out of a cake in celebration of the staff's record sales quarter.*

*Ms. Vance began to feel uncomfortable shortly after joining Diablo in February of last year. To the best of her ability, she has documented the following chronology of events:*

*1) In early March to the best of Mr. Vance's memory, this was Friday, March 5 Minot leaned in through Ms. Vance's office door and asked her to join him for drinks at the Elephant Bar. He told Ms. Vance he wanted to talk to her about a work-related issue that required her input. Vance agreed.*

*2) At the bar, Ms. Vance was surprised to see that nobody else from the office was there Minot was waiting for her alone at a table. He spoke about design and layout for a few minutes, and complimented Ms. Vance on the "new look" she was bringing to Diablo's publications. Then he asked Ms. Vance what her career plans were at Diablo and said he could be very helpful to her, because he was "an old prat buddy" of John Stamps. Ms. Vance replied that because she had just joined the company, she was unsure of her plans.*

*Minot then began to talk about how grueling the demands were at Diablo and how those demands were having an effect on his marriage. He asked Ms. Vance if she was having trouble with her own relationship because of the work schedule. Ms. Vance's reply was noncommittal; she did not feel it appropriate to talk about her personal relationships with someone at work, especially someone she did not know that well. She said she was tired and wanted to go home.*

*Minot hailed Ms. Vance a cab. After holding the door open for her, he bent to kiss her on the cheek. Ms. Vance said nothing but did not reciprocate.*

*3) Over the next few months, Minot stopped off at Ms. Vance's office once or twice a week, inviting her out to the Elephant Bar again. Ms. Vance attempted to remain noncommittal but never said absolutely "no." She never went out alone again with Minotshe has never since, in fact, been in Minot's company outside of the office for any reason.*

*4) On July 12 of last year, Ms. Vance recorded that Minot walked into her office, closed the door, and said: "We really ought to strategize about how to handle Stamps and leverage a future for you at Diablo. How about over drinks at the Elephant Bar?" When Ms. Vance declined, Minot said: "Whatever. It's your future."*

*5) On September 18, Minot's marketing staff began circulating pictures of their latest gathering, which had also included an exotic dancer. A number of people men and women on Ms. Vance's staff complained to her privately. Ms. Vance went to Minot, who promised to control his staff's behavior. At the end of the conversation, Minot laughed and said, "So I guess this means no drinks for us at the Elephant Bar?"*

*6) On October 15, Minot passed Ms. Vance in the hallway and told her that her black pantsuit looked "very hot" on her. He then wished her luck in her quarterly performance reviewwhich would be conducted by John Stamps.*

*7) Ms. Vance's October 15 performance review despite the fact that she had, within the last quarter, won a regional award for magazine design that generated quite a bit of free publicity for Diablo received an evaluation of "meets expectations," a result that did not allow her to share in the company's bonus plan.*

1. The Chief Executive Officer of Diablo Publishing is 1.____

   A. Gray Minot
   B. John Stamps
   C. Garrett Longo
   D. Mathilda Ward

2. Diablo's employment manual 2.____

   A. mentions discrimination, but not sexual harassment
   B. speaks of "harassment" only in general terms
   C. has not been revised since the company was founded
   D. explicitly forbids sexual harassment

3. The brief states that Minot has been successful in raising revenues for Diablo because he 3.____

   A. engages in unethical business practices
   B. aggressively and tirelessly seeks new clients
   C. is good at generating a strong team spirit among his employees
   D. uses his position of power to manipulate and intimidate those who work under him

4. Diablo Publishing could best be described as a(n) 4.____

   A. nationwide publisher that has a number of federal and large-chain clients
   B. small publisher of pamphlets and brochures
   C. moderately sized publisher with only one or two perennial clients
   D. large regional publisher that occupies a specific marketing niche

5. Vivian Vance began working for Diablo in the month of 5.____

   A. December
   B. January
   C. February
   D. March

6. The CEO of Diablo seems to believe that Gray Minot is 6.____

   A. the key reason why Diablo has become more successful
   B. not subject to the same employment policies as everyone else at the company
   C. placing the company at risk of more sexual harassment lawsuits
   D. a harmless "frat boy" type who needs to exercise more professional discipline

7. According to the brief, a copy of Diablo's employment manual has been circulated to 7.____

   A. only the CEO and editor-in-chief
   B. every department manager
   C. every employee who supervises another
   D. every employee

8. In the brief, each of the following dates is documented as a certainty, EXCEPT for the date when 8.____

   A. Gray Minot first asked Vivian Vance to join him at the Elephant Bar
   B. Minot proposed that they meet and "strategize" about Ms. Vance's future at Diablo
   C. Ms. Vance complained to Minot about the pictures being circulated in the office
   D. Ms. Vance's quarterly performance review with John Stamps

9. When Gray Minot first asked Vivian Vance to meet with him outside the office, the reason he gave was that he wanted to 9.____

   A. talk about how his job was affecting his marriage and personal life
   B. talk about her future plans at Diablo Publishing
   C. show her some photographs
   D. get her input on a work-related issue

10. The brief says that Vivian Vance was hired by Diablo to 10.____

   A. bring a young, attractive woman in to share an office with the older executives
   B. fulfill a gender quota
   C. bring more discipline to the design and layout staff
   D. update the look of the company's publications

11. Which of the following did NOT happen during the first meeting between Gray Minot and Vivian Vance at the Elephant Bar? 11.____

   A. Gray Minot complimented Vivian Vance's work at Diablo
   B. Vivian Vance told Gray Minot his behavior was inappropriate
   C. Gray Minot offered to help Ms. Vance advance her career
   D. Vivian Vance declined to discuss her personal life

12. When Vivian Vance complained to Minot about the behavior of his staff, his response was to 12.____

   A. tell her the photographs had nothing to do with her
   B. promise to control his staff
   C. make a vague threat about her upcoming performance review
   D. laugh it off and tell her to get over it

13. In the sequence of events described in the brief, which of the following occurred FIRST? 13.____

   A. Gray Minot entered Ms. Vance's office and closed the door
   B. Gray Minot makes an observation about Ms. Vance's pantsuit
   C. Gray Minot kissed Ms. Vance on the cheek
   D. Ms. Vance complained to Minot about his staff's behavior

14. After their first meeting at the Elephant Bar, Vivian Vance and Gray Minot 14.____

   A. met for drinks once or twice
   B. became briefly involved
   C. became bitter enemies
   D. never met outside the office again

15. When they were at the Elephant Bar and Gray Minot asked Vivian Vance about her personal life, she replied by 15.____

A. saying she was tired and wanted to go home
B. opening up to him about the strain of working for such an up-tempo business
C. telling him it was none of his business
D. changing the subject entirely

16. The brief implies that after Minot's staff circulated pictures of an exotic dancer around the office, Vivian Vance complained to him because she 16.____

A. was sick of his sexist behavior
B. was articulating the feelings of her own staff
C. was afraid Minot was unaware that he was violating the company's employment policy
D. had thought Minot really cared for her

17. The wording of the brief implies that after her performance review, Vivian Vance 17.____

A. wanted revenge on the men who were keeping her down
B. was able to share in the company's bonus plan
C. probably felt a more positive review was justified
D. resigned from Diablo Publishing

**Jimmy's Dilemma**

Francine Bodmer is a court-appointed special advocate for children in foster care in a Midwestern state. She has been assigned to resolve a dispute involving a foster child named Jimmy who has lived with his foster mother, a single woman named Elizabeth Jenkins, for the past two years. Francine has also been assigned to represent Elizabeth Jenkins' interest in court because she will not be able to attend all court appointments in New Jersey.

Jimmy, nine years old, was born and spent the first years of his life in New Jersey, but later moved to the Midwest with Ms. Jenkins. He has multiple psychological and neurological problems, including reactive attachment disorder, attention deficit/hyperactivity disorder, and Tourette's syndrome. The dispute is over the amount of money New Jersey's Office of Child Services is willing to provide for Jimmy's therapy.

On a Friday, while Jimmy is at school, Francine drives to the semi-rural home of Elizabeth Jenkins to gather facts about the dispute.

Bodmer: *Good afternoon, Ms. Jenkins. My name is Francine Bodmer and I'm here to see whether we can resolve the issue of funding for Jimmy's therapy.*

Jenkins: *Thanks for coming, Francine. I hope we can get this worked out. Please sit down.*

Bodmer: *Let me make sure I have these facts straight: Jimmy's therapist is contracted by the county agency.*

Jenkins: *That's right. Dr. Agee. He's very nice, but he says Jimmy's problems are beyond the help he can provide, and so he's referred him to a specialist in St. Louis. But New Jersey won't pay for that they want to stick with Medic-aid scale.*

Bodmer: *And to farther complicate things, the county social services agency here will not finalize adoption unless New Jersey provides the funding for these services?*

Jenkins: *That's what I've been told. Now, that's old news. Just last month I had to quit my job at the factory because of Jimmy's behavioral problems, and I have been left without medical coverage. To determine whether I can adopt Jimmy, the county said they needed a full forensic psychological evaluation for each of us. Can you imagine? It was $800 for Jimmy's test, and $1200 for mine.*

Bodmer: *And you can't pay for that.*

Jenkins: *No way!*

Bodmer: *What is the name of the person at the county agency I should speak to?*

Jenkins: *Well, I've been talking to a guy named Kevin. Kevin McDonald.*

Bodmer: *I'll tell you what. I'm going to head over to the county office right now and try to straighten this out. I'll give you a call this afternoon.*

After meeting with Kevin McDonald at the county office, Francine Bodmer telephones Jesse West, a service coordinator at New Jersey's Office of Children's Services.

West: *Hello. Jesse West here.*

Bodmer: *Hello, Mr. West. I'm Francine Bodmer, a court-appointed special advocate for Elizabeth Jenkins. Are you familiar with the case I'm referring to?*

West: (sighs) *Yeah. That one's a mess.*

Bodmer: *Well, let's try to clean it up, shall we? Can you tell me why your agency has not arranged funding for Jimmy's treatment?*

West: *We simply don't have the money and we don't think it's our responsibility, Ms. Bodmer. Jimmy lives in the Midwest now. His treatment is going to be very expensive.*

Bodmer: *Yes, but if you've read your agency policy, you know that's irrelevant. Jimmy was born in New Jersey. He was living there when he was diagnosed and placed in the system. And you how long have you worked there, Mr. West?*

West: *Three years.*

Bodmer: *So you know your agency's responsibility does not end once it runs out of funds. Have you attempted to arrange private-agency funding for Jimmy's treatment?*

West: *Well, not that I know of.*

Bodmer: *Then you admit that your work on this case is not done yet.*

West: *Ms. Bodmer, I'm going to have to speak with my boss here and get back to you on the case. I guess I'm not really sure of every detail.*

Bodmer: *That will be fine, if you' ll provide me with that person's name.*

West: *Her name is Margaret Thorson. She's Director of Child Behavioral Health Services.*

Bodmer: *I'll tell you what, Mr. West. If she's the director of those programs, I should probably be speaking directly with her, don't you think?*

West: *Yeah, probably.*

Bodmer: *Well, I'll appreciate it if you will tell her to expect my call.*

West: *I'll do that, Ms. Bodmer.*

18. Francine Bodmer is representing Elizabeth Jenkins in court because 18.____

    A. she has been ordered by the New Jersey Office of Children's Services to be Jenkins' representative
    B. Elizabeth Jenkins is not competent to represent herself
    C. Jimmy's biological mother lives in New Jersey
    D. the case is being handled by New Jersey courts, and Elizabeth Jenkins cannot attend most hearings

19. Which of the following disorders is NOT mentioned as one of Jimmy's problems? 19.____

    A. Tourette's syndrome
    B. attention deficit/hyperactivity disorder
    C. oppositional defiant disorder
    D. reactive attachment disorder

20. Jimmy has been living with Elizabeth Jenkins for ______ year(s). 20.____

    A. one
    B. two
    C. three
    D. four

21. According to Elizabeth Jenkins, Jimmy's therapist has referred him to another therapist in St. Louis because 21.____

    A. Jimmy's behavioral problems are too severe
    B. the issue of payment for his services has not yet been resolved
    C. Jimmy's adoption is being held up
    D. Jimmy's problems are more complex than the therapist can handle

22. The most important reason why Elizabeth Jenkins cannot pay for the psychological tests that were given to her and Jimmy is that she 22.____

A. had to leave her job and surrender insurance coverage
B. has been ill
C. has some behavioral problems of her own
D. recently moved from New Jersey

23. Forensic psychological tests for both Elizabeth and Jimmy were required by the 23.____

A. court in their home county
B. social services agency in their home county
C. New Jersey Office of Child Services
D. court in New Jersey

24. Jesse West is ______ with New Jersey's Office of Child Services. 24.____

A. a switchboard operator
B. a financial officer
C. a service coordinator
D. Director of Child Behavioral Services

25. In her conversation with Jesse West, Francine Bodmer implies that if his office does not have the funding to pay for Jimmy's service, it 25.____

A. is not responsible for any of the required therapy
B. should not have put him into the social service system in the first place
C. find some other way to enable Jimmy's adoption
D. has the obligation to procure the funding from another source

# KEY (CORRECT ANSWERS)

| | | | |
|---|---|---|---|
| 1. | D | 11. | B |
| 2. | D | 12. | B |
| 3. | C | 13. | C |
| 4. | D | 14. | D |
| 5. | C | 15. | A |
| 6. | A | 16. | B |
| 7. | B | 17. | C |
| 8. | A | 18. | D |
| 9. | D | 19. | C |
| 10. | D | 20. | B |

21. D
22. A
23. B
24. C
25. D

# EVALUATING CONCLUSIONS IN LIGHT OF KNOWN FACTS

## EXAMINATION SECTION

## TEST 1

DIRECTIONS: Each question or incomplete statement is followed by several suggested answers or completions. Select the one that BEST answers the question or completes the statement. *PRINT THE LETTER OF THE CORRECT ANSWER IN THE SPACE AT THE RIGHT.*

Questions 1-9.

DIRECTIONS: In Questions 1 through 9, you will read a set of facts and a conclusion drawn from them. The conclusion may be valid or invalid, based on the facts—it's your task to determine the validity of the conclusion.

For each question, select the letter before the statement that BEST expresses the relationship between the given facts and the conclusion that has been drawn from them. Your choices are:

A. The facts prove the conclusion;
B. The facts disprove the conclusion; or
C. The facts neither prove nor disprove the conclusion.

1. FACTS: If the supervisor retires, James, the assistant supervisor, will not be transferred to another department. James will be promoted to supervisor if he is not transferred. The supervisor retired. 1.____

   CONCLUSION: James will be promoted to supervisor.
   A. The facts prove the conclusion.
   B. The facts disprove the conclusion.
   C. The facts neither prove nor disprove the conclusion.

2. FACTS: In the town of Luray, every player on the softball team works at Luray National Bank. In addition, every player on the Luray softball team wear glasses. 2.____

   CONCLUSIONS: At least some of the people who work at Luray National Bank wear glasses.
   A. The facts prove the conclusion.
   B. The facts disprove the conclusion.
   C. The facts neither prove nor disprove the conclusion.

3. FACTS: The only time Henry and June go out to dinner is on an evening when they have childbirth classes. Their childbirth classes meet on Tuesdays and Thursdays. 3.____

CONCLUSION: Henry and June never go out to dinner on Friday or Saturday.
A. The facts prove the conclusion.
B. The facts disprove the conclusion.
C. The facts neither prove nor disprove the conclusion.

4. FACTS: Every player on the field hockey team has at least one bruise. Everyone on the field hockey team also has scarred knees. 4.____

CONCLUSION: Most people with both bruises and scarred knees are field hockey players.
A. The facts prove the conclusion.
B. The facts disprove the conclusion.
C. The facts neither prove nor disprove the conclusion.

5. FACTS: In the chess tournament, Lance will win his match against Jane if Jane wins her match against Mathias. If Lance wins his match against Jane, Christine will not win her match against Jane. 5.____

CONCLUSION: Christine will not win her match against Jane if Jane wins her match against Mathias.
A. The facts prove the conclusion.
B. The facts disprove the conclusion.
C. The facts neither prove nor disprove the conclusion.

6. FACTS: No green lights on the machine are indicators for the belt drive status. Not all of the lights on the machine's upper panel are green. Some lights on the machine's lower panel are green. 6.____

CONCLUSION: The green lights on the machine's lower panel may be indicators for the belt drive status.
A. The facts prove the conclusion.
B. The facts disprove the conclusion.
C. The facts neither prove nor disprove the conclusion.

7. FACTS: At a small, one-room country school, there are eight students: Amy, Ben, Carla, Dan, Elliot, Francine, Greg, and Hannah. Each student is in either the 6$^{th}$, 7$^{th}$, or 8$^{th}$ grade. Either two or three students are in each grade. Amy, Dan, and Francine are all in different grades. Ben and Elliot are both in the 7$^{th}$ grade. Hannah and Carl are in the same grade. 7.____

CONCLUSION: Exactly three students are in the 7$^{th}$ grade.
A. The facts prove the conclusion.
B. The facts disprove the conclusion.
C. The facts neither prove nor disprove the conclusion.

8. <u>FACTS:</u> Two married couples are having lunch together. Two of the four people are German and two are Russian, but in each couple the nationality of the spouse is not necessarily the same as the other's. One person in the group is a teacher, the other a lawyer, one an engineer, and the other a writer. The teacher is a Russian man. The writer is Russian, and her husband is an engineer. One of the people, Mr. Stern, is German. 8.____

<u>CONCLUSION:</u> Mr. Stern's wife is a writer.
A. The facts prove the conclusion.
B. The facts disprove the conclusion.
C. The facts neither prove nor disprove the conclusion.

9. <u>FACTS:</u> The flume ride at the county fair is open only to children who are at least 36 inches tall. Lisa is 30 inches tall. John is shorter than Henry, but more than 10 inches taller than Lisa. 9.____

<u>CONCLUSION:</u> Lisa is the only one who can't ride the flume ride.
A. The facts prove the conclusion.
B. The facts disprove the conclusion.
C. The facts neither prove nor disprove the conclusion.

Questions 10-17.

DIRECTIONS: Questions 10 through 17 are based on the following reading passage. It is not your knowledge of the particular topic that is being tested, but your ability to reason based on what you have read. The passage is likely to detail several proposed courses of action and factors affecting these proposals. The reading passage is followed by a conclusion or outcome based on the facts in the passage, or a description of a decision taken regarding the situation. The conclusion is followed by a number of statements that have a possible connection to the conclusion. For each statement, you are to determine whether:
A. The statement proves the conclusion.
B. The statement supports the conclusion but does not prove it.
C. The statement disproves the conclusion.
D. The statement weakens the conclusion but does not disprove it.
E. The statement has no relevance to the conclusion.

Remember that the conclusion after the passage is to be accepted as the outcome of what actually happened, and that you are being asked to evaluate the impact each statement would have had on the conclusion.

PASSAGE:

The Grand Army of Foreign Wars, a national veteran's organization, is struggling to maintain its National Home, where the widowed spouses and orphans of deceased members are housed together in a small village-like community. The Home is open to spouses and children who are bereaved for any reason, regardless of whether the member's death was related to military service, but a new global conflict has led to a dramatic surge in the number of members' deaths: many veterans who re-enlisted for the conflict have been killed in action.

The Grand Army of Foreign Wars is considering several options for handling the increased number of applications for housing at the National Home, which has been traditionally supported by membership due. At its national convention, it will choose only one of the following:

The first idea is a one-time $50 tax on all members, above and beyond the dues they pay already. Since the organization has more than a million member, this tax should be sufficient for the construction and maintenance of new housing for applicants on the existing grounds of the National Home. The idea is opposed, however, by some older members who live on fixed incomes. These members object in principle to the taxation of Grand Army members. The Grand Army has never imposed a tax on its members.

The second idea is to launch a national fundraising drive the public relations campaign that will attract donations for the National Home. Several national celebrities are members of the organization, and other celebrities could be attracted to the cause. Many Grand Army members are wary of this approach, however: in the past, the net receipts of some fundraising efforts have been relatively insignificant, given the costs of staging them.

A third approach, suggested by many of the younger members, is to have new applicants share some of the costs of construction and maintenance. The spouses and children would pay an up-front "enrollment" fee, based on a sliding scale proportionate to their income and assets, and then a monthly fee adjusted similarly to contribute to maintenance costs. Many older members are strongly opposed to this idea, as it is in direct contradiction to the principles on which the organization was founded more than a century ago.

The fourth option is simply to maintain the status quo, focus the organization's efforts on supporting the families who already live at the National Home, and wait to accept new applicants based on attrition.

CONCLUSION: At its annual national convention, the Grand Army of Foreign Wars votes to impose a one-time tax of $10 on each member for the purpose of expanding and supporting the National Home to welcome a larger number of applicants. The tax is considered to be the solution most likely to produce the funds needed to accommodate the growing number of applicants.

10. Actuarial studies have shown that because the Grand Army's membership consists mostly of older veterans from earlier wars, the organization's membership will suffer a precipitous decline in numbers in about five years. 10.____
    A. The statement proves the conclusion.
    B. The statement supports the conclusion but does not prove it.
    C. The statement disproves the conclusion.
    D. The statement weakens the conclusion but does not disprove it.
    E. The statement has no relevance to the conclusion.

11. After passage of the funding measure, a splinter group of older members appeals for the "sliding scale" provision to be applied to the tax, so that some members may be allowed to contribute less based on their income. 11.____
    A. The statement proves the conclusion.
    B. The statement supports the conclusion but does not prove it.
    C. The statement disproves the conclusion.
    D. The statement weakens the conclusion but does not disprove it.
    E. The statement has no relevance to the conclusion.

12. The original charter of the Grand Army of Foreign Wars specifically states that the organization will not levy taxes or duties on its members beyond its modest annual dues. It takes a super-majority of attending delegates at the national convention to make alterations to the charter. 12.____
    A. The statement proves the conclusion.
    B. The statement supports the conclusion but does not prove it.
    C. The statement disproves the conclusion.
    D. The statement weakens the conclusion but does not disprove it.
    E. The statement has no relevance to the conclusion.

13. Six months before Grand Army of Foreign Wars' national convention, the Internal Revenue Service rules that because it is an organization that engages in political lobbying, the Grand Army must no longer enjoy its own federal tax-exempt status. 13.____
    A. The statement proves the conclusion.
    B. The statement supports the conclusion but does not prove it.
    C. The statement disproves the conclusion.
    D. The statement weakens the conclusion but does not disprove it.
    E. The statement has no relevance to the conclusion.

14. Two months before the national convention, Dirk Rockwell, arguably the country's most famous film actor, announces in a nationally televised interview that he has been saddened to learn of the plight of the National Home, and that he is going to make it his own personal crusade to see that it is able to house and support a greater number of widowed spouses and orphans in the future. 14.____
    A. The statement proves the conclusion.
    B. The statement supports the conclusion but does not prove it.
    C. The statement disproves the conclusion.
    D. The statement weakens the conclusion but does not disprove it.
    E. The statement has no relevance to the conclusion.

15. The Grand Army's final estimate is that the cost of expanding the National Home to accommodate the increased number of applicants will be about $61 million. 15.____
    A. The statement proves the conclusion.
    B. The statement supports the conclusion but does not prove it.
    C. The statement disproves the conclusion.
    D. The statement weakens the conclusion but does not disprove it.
    E. The statement has no relevance to the conclusion.

16. Just before the national convention, the Federal Department of Veterans Affairs announces steep cuts in the benefits package that is currently offered to the widowed spouses and orphans of veterans. 16.____
    A. The statement proves the conclusion.
    B. The statement supports the conclusion but does not prove it.
    C. The statement disproves the conclusion.
    D. The statement weakens the conclusion but does not disprove it.
    E. The statement has no relevance to the conclusion.

17. After the national convention, the Grand Army of Foreign Wars begins charging a modest "start-up" fee to all families who apply for residence at the national home. 17.____
   A. The statement proves the conclusion.
   B. The statement supports the conclusion but does not prove it.
   C. The statement disproves the conclusion.
   D. The statement weakens the conclusion but does not disprove it.
   E. The statement has no relevance to the conclusion.

Questions 18-25.

DIRECTIONS: Questions 18 through 25 each provide four factual statements and a conclusion based on these statements. After reading the entire question, you will decide whether:
   A. The conclusion is proved by statements I-IV;
   B. The conclusion is disproved by statements I-IV.
   C. The facts are not sufficient to prove or disprove the conclusion.

18. <u>FACTUAL STATEMENTS:</u> 18.____
   I. In the Field Day high jump competition, Martha jumped higher than Frank.
   II. Carl jumped higher than Ignacio.
   III. Ignacio jumped higher than Frank.
   IV. Dan jumped higher than Carl.

   <u>CONCLUSION:</u> Frank finished last in the high jump competition.
   A. The conclusion is proved by statements I-IV;
   B. The conclusion is disproved by statements I-IV.
   C. The facts are not sufficient to prove or disprove the conclusion.

19. <u>FACTUAL STATEMENTS:</u> 19.____
   I. The door to the hammer mill chamber is locked if light 6 is red.
   II. The door to the hammer mill chamber is locked only when the mill is operating.
   III. If the mill is not operating, light 6 is blue.
   IV. Light 6 is blue.

   <u>CONCLUSION:</u> The door to the hammer mill chamber is locked.
   A. The conclusion is proved by statements I-IV;
   B. The conclusion is disproved by statements I-IV.
   C. The facts are not sufficient to prove or disprove the conclusion.

20. <u>FACTUAL STATEMENTS:</u> 20.____
   I. Ziegfried, the lion tamer at the circus, has demanded ten additional minutes of performance time during each show.
   II. If Ziegfried is allowed his ten additional minutes per show, he will attempt to teach Kimba the tiger to shoot a basketball.
   III. If Kimba learns how to shoot a basketball, then Ziegfried was not given his ten additional minutes.
   IV. Ziegfried was given his ten additional minutes.

CONCLUSION: Despite Ziegfried's efforts, Kimba did not learn how to shoot a basketball.

A. The conclusion is proved by statements I-IV;
B. The conclusion is disproved by statements I-IV.
C. The facts are not sufficient to prove or disprove the conclusion.

21. FACTUAL STATEMENTS: 21.____

I. If Stan goes to counseling, Sara won't divorce him.
II. If Sara divorces Stan, she'll move back to Texas.
III. If Sara doesn't divorce Stan, Irene will be disappointed.
IV. Stan goes to counseling.

CONCLUSION: Irene will be disappointed.

A. The conclusion is proved by statements I-IV;
B. The conclusion is disproved by statements I-IV.
C. The facts are not sufficient to prove or disprove the conclusion.

22. FACTUAL STATEMENTS: 22.____

I. If Delia is promoted to district manager, Claudia will have to be promoted to team leader.
II. Delia will be promoted to district manager unless she misses her fourth-quarter sales quota.
III. If Claudia is promoted to team leader, Thomas will be promoted to assistant team leader.
IV. Delia meets her fourth-quarter sales quota.

CONCLUSION: Thomas is promoted to assistant team leader.

A. The conclusion is proved by statements I-IV;
B. The conclusion is disproved by statements I-IV.
C. The facts are not sufficient to prove or disprove the conclusion.

23. FACTUAL STATEMENTS: 23.____

I. Clone D is identical to Clone B.
II. Clone B is not identical to Clone A.
III. Clone D is not identical to Clone C.
IV. Clone E is not identical to the clones that are identical to Clone B.

CONCLUSION: Clone E is identical to Clone D.

A. The conclusion is proved by statements I-IV;
B. The conclusion is disproved by statements I-IV.
C. The facts are not sufficient to prove or disprove the conclusion.

24. FACTUAL STATEMENTS: 24.____

I. In the Stafford Tower, each floor is occupied by a single business.
II. Big G Staffing is on a floor between CyberGraphics and MainEvent.
III. Gasco is on the floor directly below CyberGraphics and three floors above Treehorn Audio.
IV. MainEvent is five floors below EZ Tax and four floors below Treehorn Audio.

CONCLUSION: EZ Tax is on a floor between Gasco and MainEvent.
A. The conclusion is proved by statements I-IV;
B. The conclusion is disproved by statements I-IV.
C. The facts are not sufficient to prove or disprove the conclusion.

25. FACTUAL STATEMENTS: 25.____
I. Only county roads lead to Nicodemus.
II. All the roads from Hill City to Graham County are federal highways.
III. Some of the roads from Plainville lead to Nicodemus.
IV. Some of the roads running from Hill City lead to Strong City.

CONCLUSION: Some of the roads from Plainville are county roads.
A. The conclusion is proved by statements I-IV;
B. The conclusion is disproved by statements I-IV.
C. The facts are not sufficient to prove or disprove the conclusion.

---

## KEY (CORRECT ANSWERS)

1. A
2. A
3. A
4. C
5. A

6. B
7. A
8. A
9. A
10. E

11. A
12. D
13. E
14. D
15. B

16. B
17. C
18. A
19. B
20. A

21. A
22. A
23. B
24. A
25. A

# SOLUTIONS TO PROBLEMS

1. CORRECT ANSWER: A
Given Statement 3, we deduce that James will not be transferred to another department. By Statement 2, we can conclude that James will be promoted.

2. CORRECT ANSWER: A
Since every player on the softball team wears glasses, these individuals compose some of the people who work at the bank. Although not every person who works at the bank plays softball, those bank employees who do play softball wear glasses.

3. CORRECT ANSWER: A
If Henry and June go out to dinner, we conclude that it must be on Tuesday or Thursday, which are the only two days when they have childbirth classes. This implies that if it is not Tuesday or Thursday, then this couple does not go out to dinner.

4. CORRECT ANSWER: C
We can only conclude that if a person plays on the field hockey team, then he or she has both bruises and scarred knees. But there are probably a great number of people who have both bruises and scarred knees but do not play on the field hockey team. The given conclusion can neither be proven or disproven.

5. CORRECT ANSWER: A
From statement 1, if Jane beats Mathias, then Lance will beat Jane. Using statement 2, we can then conclude that Christine will not win her match against Jane.

6. CORRECT ANSWER: B
Statement 1 tells us that no green light can be an indicator of the belt drive status. Thus, the given conclusion must be false.

7. CORRECT ANSWER: A
We already know that Ben and Elliot are in the $7^{th}$ grade. Even though Hannah and Carl are in the same grade, it cannot be the $7^{th}$ grade because we would then have at least four students in this $7^{th}$ grade. This would contradict the third statement, which states that either two or three students are in each grade. Since Amy, Dan, and Francine are in different grade, exactly one of them must be in the $7^{th}$ grade. Thus, Ben, Elliot, and exactly one of Amy, Dan, and Francine are the three students in the $7^{th}$ grade.

8. CORRECT ANSWER: A
One man is a teacher, who is Russian. We know that the writer is female and is Russian. Since her husband is an engineer, he cannot be the Russian teacher. Thus, her husband is of German descent, namely Mr. Stern. This means that Mr. Stern's wife is the writer. Note that one couple consists of a male Russian teacher and a female German lawyer. The other couple consists of a male German engineer and a female Russian writer.

9. CORRECT ANSWER: A
Since John is more than 10 inches taller than Lisa, his height is at least 46 inches. Also, John is shorter than Henry, so Henry's height must be greater than 46 inches. Thus, Lisa is the only one whose height is less than 36 inches. Therefore, she is the only one who is not allowed on the flume ride.

18. CORRECT ANSWER: A
Dan jumped higher than Carl, who jumped higher than Ignacio, who jumped higher than Frank. Since Martha jumped higher than Frank, every person jumped higher than Frank. Thus, Frank finished last.

19. CORRECT ANSWER: B
If the light is red, then the door is locked. If the door is locked, then the mill is operating. Reversing the logical sequence of these statements, if the mill is not operating, then the door is not locked, which means that the light is blue. Thus, the given conclusion is disproved.

20. CORRECT ANSWER: A
Using the contrapositive of statement III, Ziegfried was given his ten additional minutes, then Kimba did not learn how to shoot a basketball. Since statement IV is factual, the conclusion is proved.

21. CORRECT ANSWER: A
From Statements IV and I, we conclude that Sara doesn't divorce Stan. Then statement III reveals that Irene will be disappointed. Thus, the conclusion is proved.

22. CORRECT ANSWER: A
Statement II can be rewritten as "Delia is promoted to district manager or she misses her sales quota." Furthermore, this statement is equivalent to "If Delia makes her sales quota, then she is promoted to district manager." From statement I, we conclude that Claudia is promoted to team leader. Finally, by statement III, Thomas is promoted to assistant team leader.

23. CORRECT ANSWER: B
By statement IV, Clone E is not identical to any clones identical to Clone B. Statement I tells us that Clones B and D are identical. Therefore, Clone E cannot be identical to Clone D. The conclusion is disproved.

24. CORRECT ANSWER: A
Based on all four statements, CyberGraphics is somewhere below MainEvent. Gasco is one floor below CyberGraphics. EZ Tax is two floors below Gasco. Treehorn Audio is one floor below EZ Tax. MainEvent is four floors below Treehorn Audio. Thus, EZ Tax is two floors below Gasco and five floors above MainEvent. The conclusion is proved.

25. CORRECT ANSWER: A
From statement III, we know that some of the roads from Plainville lead to Nicodemus. But statement I tells us that only county roads lead to Nicodemus. Therefore, some of the roads from Plainville must be county roads. The conclusion is proved.

# TEST 2

DIRECTIONS: Each question or incomplete statement is followed by several suggested answers or completions. Select the one that BEST answers the question or completes the statement. *PRINT THE LETTER OF THE CORRECT ANSWER IN THE SPACE AT THE RIGHT.*

Questions 1-9.

DIRECTIONS: In Questions 1 through 9, you will read a set of facts and a conclusion drawn from them. The conclusion may be valid or invalid, based on the facts—it's your task to determine the validity of the conclusion.

For each question, select the letter before the statement that BEST expresses the relationship between the given facts and the conclusion that has been drawn from them. Your choices are:

A. The facts prove the conclusion;
B. The facts disprove the conclusion; or
C. The facts neither prove nor disprove the conclusion.

1. FACTS: Some employees in the testing department are statisticians. Most of the statisticians who work in the testing department are projection specialists. Tom Wilks works in the testing department. 1.____

   CONCLUSION: Tom Wilks is a statistician.
   A. The facts prove the conclusion.
   B. The facts disprove the conclusion.
   C. The facts neither prove nor disprove the conclusion.

2. FACTS: Ten coins are split among Hank, Lawrence, and Gail. If Lawrence gives his coins to Hank, then Hank will have more coins than Gail. If Gail gives her coins to Lawrence, then Lawrence will have more coins than Hank. 2.____

   CONCLUSION: Hank has six coins.
   A. The facts prove the conclusion.
   B. The facts disprove the conclusion.
   C. The facts neither prove nor disprove the conclusion.

3. FACTS: Nobody loves everybody. Janet loves Ken. Ken loves everybody who loves Janet. 3.____

   CONCLUSION: Everybody loves Janet.
   A. The facts prove the conclusion.
   B. The facts disprove the conclusion.
   C. The facts neither prove nor disprove the conclusion.

4. FACTS: Most of the Torres family lives in East Los Angeles. Many people in East Los Angeles celebrate Cinco de Mayo. Joe is a member of the Torres family. 4.____

CONCLUSION: Joe lives in East Los Angeles.
A. The facts prove the conclusion.
B. The facts disprove the conclusion.
C. The facts neither prove nor disprove the conclusion.

5. FACTS: Five professionals each occupy one story of a five-story office building. Dr. Kane's office is above Dr. Assad's. Dr. Johnson's office is between Dr. Kane's and Dr. Conlon's. Dr. Steen's office is between Dr. Conlon's and Dr. Assad's. Dr. Johnson is on the fourth story. 5.____

CONCLUSION: Dr. Kane occupies the top story.
A. The facts prove the conclusion.
B. The facts disprove the conclusion.
C. The facts neither prove nor disprove the conclusion.

6. FACTS: To be eligible for membership in the Yukon Society, a person must be able to either tunnel through a snowbank while wearing only a T-shirt and short, or hold his breath for two minutes under water that is 50°F. Ray can only hold his breath for a minute and a half. 6.____

CONCLUSION: Ray can still become a member of the Yukon Society by tunneling through a snowbank while wearing a T-shirt and shorts.
A. The facts prove the conclusion.
B. The facts disprove the conclusion.
C. The facts neither prove nor disprove the conclusion.

7. FACTS: A mark is worth five plunks. You can exchange four sharps for a tinplot. It takes eight marks to buy a sharp. 7.____

CONCLUSION: A sharp is the most valuable.
A. The facts prove the conclusion.
B. The facts disprove the conclusion.
C. The facts neither prove nor disprove the conclusion.

8. FACTS: There are gibbons, as well as lemurs, who like to play in the trees at the monkey house. All those who like to play in the trees at the monkey house are fed lettuce and bananas. 8.____

CONCLUSION: Lemurs and gibbons are types of monkeys.
A. The facts prove the conclusion.
B. The facts disprove the conclusion.
C. The facts neither prove nor disprove the conclusion.

9. FACTS: None of the Blackfoot tribes is a Salishan Indian tribe. Salishan Indians came from the northern Pacific Coast. All Salishan Indians live each of the Continental Divide. 9.____

CONCLUSION: No Blackfoot tribes live east of the Continental Divide.
A. The facts prove the conclusion.
B. The facts disprove the conclusion.
C. The facts neither prove nor disprove the conclusion.

Questions 10-17.

DIRECTIONS: Questions 10 through 17 are based on the following reading passage. It is not your knowledge of the particular topic that is being tested, but your ability to reason based on what you have read. The passage is likely to detail several proposed courses of action and factors affecting these proposals. The reading passage is followed by a conclusion or outcome based on the facts in the passage, or a description of a decision taken regarding the situation. The conclusion is followed by a number of statements that have a possible connection to the conclusion. For each statement, you are to determine whether:
A. The statement proves the conclusion.
B. The statement supports the conclusion but does not prove it.
C. The statement disproves the conclusion.
D. The statement weakens the conclusion but does not disprove it.
E. The statement has no relevance to the conclusion.

Remember that the conclusion after the passage is to be accepted as the outcome of what actually happened, and that you are being asked to evaluate the impact each statement would have had on the conclusion.

PASSAGE:

On August 12, Beverly Willey reported that she was in the elevator late on the previous evening after leaving her office on the 16th floor of a large office building. In her report, she states that a man got on the elevator at the 11th floor, pulled her off the elevator, assaulted her, and stole her purse. Ms. Willey reported that she had seen the man in the elevators and hallways of the building before. She believes that the man works in the building. Her description of him is as follows: he is tall, unshaven, with wavy brown hair and a scar on his left cheek. He walks with a pronounced limp, often dragging his left foot behind his right.

CONCLUSION: After Beverly Willey makes her report, the police arrest a 43-year-old man, Barton Black, and charge him with her assault.

10. Barton Black is a former Marine who served in Vietnam, where he sustained shrapnel wounds to the left side of his face and suffered nerve damage in his left leg. 10.____
   A. The statement proves the conclusion.
   B. The statement supports the conclusion but does not prove it.
   C. The statement disproves the conclusion.
   D. The statement weakens the conclusion but does not disprove it.
   E. The statement has no relevance to the conclusion.

11. When they arrived at his residence to question him, detectives were greeted at the door by Barton Black, who was tall and clean-shaven. 11.____
   A. The statement proves the conclusion.
   B. The statement supports the conclusion but does not prove it.
   C. The statement disproves the conclusion.
   D. The statement weakens the conclusion but does not disprove it.
   E. The statement has no relevance to the conclusion.

12. Barton Black was booked into the county jail several days after Beverly Willey's assault. 12.____
   A. The statement proves the conclusion.
   B. The statement supports the conclusion but does not prove it.
   C. The statement disproves the conclusion.
   D. The statement weakens the conclusion but does not disprove it.
   E. The statement has no relevance to the conclusion.

13. Upon further investigation, detectives discover that Beverly Willey does not work at the office building. 13.____
   A. The statement proves the conclusion.
   B. The statement supports the conclusion but does not prove it.
   C. The statement disproves the conclusion.
   D. The statement weakens the conclusion but does not disprove it.
   E. The statement has no relevance to the conclusion.

14. Upon further investigation, detectives discover that Barton Black does not work at the office building. 14.____
   A. The statement proves the conclusion.
   B. The statement supports the conclusion but does not prove it.
   C. The statement disproves the conclusion.
   D. The statement weakens the conclusion but does not disprove it.
   E. The statement has no relevance to the conclusion.

15. In the spring of the following year, Barton Black is convicted of assaulting Beverly Willey on August 11. 15.____
   A. The statement proves the conclusion.
   B. The statement supports the conclusion but does not prove it.
   C. The statement disproves the conclusion.
   D. The statement weakens the conclusion but does not disprove it.
   E. The statement has no relevance to the conclusion.

16. During their investigation of the assault, detectives determine that Beverly Willey was assaulted on the 12th floor of the office building. 16.____
    A. The statement proves the conclusion.
    B. The statement supports the conclusion but does not prove it.
    C. The statement disproves the conclusion.
    D. The statement weakens the conclusion but does not disprove it.
    E. The statement has no relevance to the conclusion.

17. The day after Beverly Willey's assault, Barton Black fled the area and was never seen again. 17.____
    A. The statement proves the conclusion.
    B. The statement supports the conclusion but does not prove it.
    C. The statement disproves the conclusion.
    D. The statement weakens the conclusion but does not disprove it.
    E. The statement has no relevance to the conclusion.

Questions 18-25.

DIRECTIONS: Questions 18 through 25 each provide four factual statements and a conclusion based on these statements. After reading the entire question, you will decide whether:
A. The conclusion is proved by statements I-IV;
B. The conclusion is disproved by statements I-IV.
C. The facts are not sufficient to prove or disprove the conclusion.

18. FACTUAL STATEMENTS: 18.____
    I. Among five spice jars on the shelf, the sage is to the right of the parsley.
    II. The pepper is to the left of the basil.
    III. The nutmeg is between the sage and the pepper.
    IV. The pepper is the second spice from the left.

    CONCLUSION: The safe is the farthest to the right.
    A. The conclusion is proved by statements I-IV;
    B. The conclusion is disproved by statements I-IV.
    C. The facts are not sufficient to prove or disprove the conclusion.

19. FACTUAL STATEMENTS: 19.____
    I. Gear X rotates in a clockwise direction if Switch C is in the OFF position.
    II. Gear X will rotate in a counter-clockwise direction is Switch C is ON.
    III. If Gear X is rotating in a clockwise direction, then Gear Y will not be rotating at all.
    IV. Switch C is ON.

    CONCLUSION: Gear X is rotating in a counter-clockwise direction.
    A. The conclusion is proved by statements I-IV;
    B. The conclusion is disproved by statements I-IV.
    C. The facts are not sufficient to prove or disprove the conclusion.

20. FACTUAL STATEMENTS: 20.____
I. Lane will leave for the Toronto meeting today only if Terence, Rourke, and Jackson all file their marketing reports by the end of the work day.
II. Rourke will file her report on time only if Ganz submits last quarter's data.
III. If Terence attends the security meeting, he will attend it with Jackson, and they will not file their marketing reports by the end of the work day.

CONCLUSION: Lane will leave for the Toronto meeting today.
A. The conclusion is proved by statements I-IV;
B. The conclusion is disproved by statements I-IV.
C. The facts are not sufficient to prove or disprove the conclusion.

21. FACTUAL STATEMENTS: 21.____
I. Bob is in second place in the Boston Marathon.
II. Gregory is winning the Boston Marathon.
III. There are four miles to go in the race, and Bob is gaining on Gregory at the rate of 100 yards every minute.
IV. There are 1760 yards in a mile and Gregory's usual pace during the Boston Marathon is one mile every six minutes.

CONCLUSION: Bob wins the Boston Marathon.
A. The conclusion is proved by statements I-IV;
B. The conclusion is disproved by statements I-IV.
C. The facts are not sufficient to prove or disprove the conclusion.

22. FACTUAL STATEMENTS: 22.____
I. Four brothers are named Earl, John, Gary, and Pete.
II. Earl and Pete are unmarried.
III. John is shorter than the youngest of the four.
IV. The oldest brother is married, and is also the tallest.

CONCLUSION: Gary is the oldest brother.
A. The conclusion is proved by statements I-IV;
B. The conclusion is disproved by statements I-IV.
C. The facts are not sufficient to prove or disprove the conclusion.

23. FACTUAL STATEMENTS: 23.____
I. Brigade X is ten miles from the demilitarized zone.
II. If General Woundwort gives the order, Brigade X will advance to the demilitarized zone, but not quickly enough to reach the zone before the conflict begins.
III. Brigade Y, five miles behind Brigade X, will not advance unless General Woundwort gives the order.
IV. Brigade Y advances.

CONCLUSION: Brigade X reaches the demilitarized zone before the conflict begins.

A. The conclusion is proved by statements I-IV;
B. The conclusion is disproved by statements I-IV.
C. The facts are not sufficient to prove or disprove the conclusion.

24. FACTUAL STATEMENTS: 24.____

I. Jerry has decided to take a cab from Fullerton to Elverton.
II. Chubby Cab charges $5 plus $3 a mile.
III. Orange Cab charges $7.50 but gives free mileage for the first 5 miles.
IV. After the first 5 miles, Orange Cab charges $2.50 a mile.

CONCLUSION: Orange Cab is the cheaper fare from Fullerton to Elverton.

A. The conclusion is proved by statements I-IV;
B. The conclusion is disproved by statements I-IV.
C. The facts are not sufficient to prove or disprove the conclusion.

25. FACTUAL STATEMENTS: 25.____

I. Dan is never in class when his friend Lucy is absent.
II. Lucy is never absent unless her mother is sick.
III. If Lucy is in class, Sergio is in class also.
IV. Sergio is never in class when Dalton is absent.

CONCLUSION: If Lucy is absent, Dalton may be in class.

A. The conclusion is proved by statements I-IV;
B. The conclusion is disproved by statements I-IV.
C. The facts are not sufficient to prove or disprove the conclusion.

# KEY (CORRECT ANSWERS)

1. C
2. B
3. B
4. C
5. A

6. A
7. B
8. C
9. C
10. B

11. E
12. B
13. D
14. E
15. A

16. E
17. C
18. B
19. A
20. C

21. C
22. A
23. B
24. A
25. B

# SOLUTIONS TO PROBLEMS

1. CORRECT ANSWER: C
Statement 1 only tells us that some employees who work in the Testing Department are statisticians. This means that we need to allow the possibility that at least one person in this department is not a statistician. Thus, if a person works in the Testing Department, we cannot conclude whether or not this individual is a statistician.

2. CORRECT ANSWER: B
If Hank had six coins, then the total of Gail's collection and Lawrence's collection would be four. Thus, if Gail gave all her coins to Lawrence, Lawrence would only have four coins. Thus, it would be impossible for Lawrence to have more coins than Hank.

3. CORRECT ANSWER: B
Statement 1 tells us that nobody loves everybody. If everybody loved Janet, then Statement 3 would imply that Ken loves everybody. This would contradict statement 1. The conclusion is disproved.

4. CORRECT ANSWER: C
Although most of the Torres family lives in East Los Angeles, we can assume that some members of this family do not live in East Los Angeles. Thus, we cannot prove or disprove that Joe, who is a member of the Torres family, lives in East Los Angeles.

5. CORRECT ANSWER: A
Since Dr. Johnson is on the 4$^{th}$ floor, either (a) Dr. Kane is on the 5$^{th}$ floor and Dr. Conlon is on the 3$^{rd}$ floor, or (b) Dr. Kane is on the 3$^{rd}$ floor and Dr. Conlon is on the 5$^{th}$ floor. If option (b) were correct, then since Dr. Assad would be on the 1$^{st}$ floor, it would be impossible for Dr. Steen's office to be between Dr. Conlon and Dr. Assad's office. Therefore, Dr. Kane's office must be on the 5$^{th}$ floor. The order of the doctors' offices, from 5$^{th}$ floor down to the 1$^{st}$ floor is: Dr. Kane, Dr. Johnson, Dr. Conlon, Dr. Steen, Dr. Assad.

6. CORRECT ANSWER: A
Ray does not satisfy the requirement of holding his breath for two minutes under water, since he can only hold is breath for one minute in that setting. But if he tunnels through a snowbank with just a T-shirt and shorts, he will satisfy the eligibility requirement. Note that the eligibility requirement contains the key word "or." So only one of the two clauses separated by "or" need to be fulfilled.

7. CORRECT ANSWER: B
Statement 2 says that four sharps is equivalent to one tinplot. This means that a tinplot is worth more than a sharp. The conclusion is disproved. We note that the order of these items, from most valuable to least valuable are: tinplot, sharp, mark, plunk.

8. CORRECT ANSWER: C
We can only conclude that gibbons and lemurs are fed lettuce and bananas. We can neither prove nor disprove that these animals are types of monkeys.

9. CORRECT ANSWER: C
We know that all Salishan Indians live east of the Continental Divide. But some non-members of this tribe of Indians may also live east of the Continental Divide. Since none of the members of the Blackfoot tribe belong to the Salishan Indian tribe, we cannot draw any conclusion about the location of the Blackfoot tribe with respect to the Continental Divide.

18. CORRECT ANSWER: B
Since the pepper is second from the left and the nutmeg is between the sage and the pepper, the positions 2, 3, and 4 (from the left) are pepper, nutmeg, sage. By statement II, the basil must be in position 5, which implies that the parsley is in position 1. Therefore, the basil, not the sage, is farthest to the right. The conclusion disproved.

19. CORRECT ANSWER: A
Statement II assures us that if switch C is ON, then Gear X is rotating in a counterclockwise direction. The conclusion is proved.

20. CORRECT ANSWER: C
Based on Statement IV, followed by Statement II, we conclude that Ganz and Rourke will file their reports on time. Statement III reveals that if Terence and Jackson attend the security meeting, they will fail to file their reports on time. We have no further information if Terence and Jackson attended the security meeting, so we are not able to either confirm or deny that their reports were filed on time. This implies that we cannot know for certain that Lane will leave for his meeting in Toronto.

21. CORRECT ANSWER: C
Although Bob is in second place behind Gregory, we cannot deduce how far behind Gregory he is running. At Gregory's current pace, he will cover four miles in 24 minutes. If Bob were only 100 yards behind Gregory, he would catch up to Gregory in one minute. But if Bob were very far behind Gregory, for example 5 miles, this is the equivalent of (5)(1760) = 8800 yards. Then Bob would need 8800/100 = 88 minutes to catch up to Gregory. Thus, the given facts are not sufficient to draw a conclusion.

22. CORRECT ANSWER: A
Statement II tells us that neither Earl nor Pete could be the oldest; also, either John or Gary is married. Statement IV reveals that the oldest brother is both married and the tallest. By Statement III, John cannot be the tallest. Since John is not the tallest, he is not the oldest. Thus, the oldest brother must be Gary. The conclusion is proved.

23. CORRECT ANSWER: B
By Statements III and IV, General Woundwort must have given the order to advance. Statement II then tells us that Brigade X will advance to the demilitarized zone, but not soon enough before the conflict begins. Thus, the conclusion is disproved.

24. CORRECT ANSWER: A
If the distance is 5 miles or less, then the cost for the Orange Cab is only $7.50, whereas the cost for the Chubby Cab is $5 + 3x, where x represents the number of miles traveled. For 1 to 5 miles, the cost of the Chubby Cab is between $8 and $20. This means that for a distance of 5 miles, the Orange Cab costs $7.50, whereas the Chubby Cab costs $20. After 5 miles, the cost per mile of the Chubby Cab exceeds the cost per mile of the Orange Cab. Thus, regardless of the actual distance between Fullerton and Elverton, the cost for the Orange Cab will be cheaper than that of the Chubby Cab.

25. CORRECT ANSWER: B
It looks like "Dalton" should be replaced by "Dan" in the conclusion. Then by statement I, if Lucy is absent, Dan is never in class. Thus, the conclusion is disproved.

# EVALUATING INFORMATION AND EVIDENCE

## EXAMINATION SECTION

## TEST 1

DIRECTIONS: Each question or incomplete statement is followed by several suggested answers or completions. Select the one that BEST answers the question or completes the statement. *PRINT THE LETTER OF THE CORRECT ANSWER IN THE SPACE AT THE RIGHT.*

Questions 1-9.

DIRECTIONS: Questions 1 through 9 measure your ability to (1) determine whether statements from witnesses say essentially the same thing and (2) determine the evidence needed to make it reasonably certain that a particular conclusion is true.

1. Which of the following pairs of statements say essentially the same thing in two different ways? 1.____
   I. Some employees at the water department have fully vested pensions.
   At least one employee at the water department has a pension that is not fully vested.
   II. All swans are white birds.
   A bird that is not white is not a swan.
   The CORRECT answer is:
   A. I only B. I and II C. II only D. Neither I nor II

2. Which of the following pairs of statements say essentially the same thing in two different ways? 2.____
   I. If you live in Humboldt County, your property taxes are high.
   If your property taxes are high, you live in Humboldt County.
   II. All the Hutchinsons live in Lindsborg.
   At least some Hutchinsons do not live in Lindsborg.
   The CORRECT answer is;
   A. I only B. I and II C. II only D. Neither I nor II

3. Which of the following pairs of statements say essentially the same thing in two different ways? 3.____
   I. Although Spike is a friendly dog, he is also one of the most unpopular dogs on the block.
   Although Spike is one of the most unpopular dogs on the block, he is a friendly dog.
   II. Everyone in Precinct 19 is taller than Officer Banks.
   Nobody in Precinct 19 is shorter than Officer Banks.
   The CORRECT answer is:
   A. I only B. I and II C. II only D. Neither I nor II

4. Which of the following pairs of statements say essentially the same thing in two different ways? 4.____

I. On Friday, every officer in Precinct 1 is assigned parking duty or crowd control, or both.
If a Precinct 1 officer has been assigned neither parking duty nor crowd control, it is not Friday.

II. Because the farmer mowed the hay fields today, his house will have mice tomorrow.
Whenever the farmer mows his hay fields, his house has mice the next day.

The CORRECT answer is:

A. I only B. I and II C. II only D. Neither I nor II

5. <u>Summary of Evidence Collected to Date</u>: 5.____

I. Fishing in the Little Pony River is against the law.
Captain Rick caught an 8-inch trout and ate it for dinner.

<u>Prematurely Drawn Conclusion</u>: Captain Rick broke the law.

Which of the following pieces of evidence, if any, would make it reasonably certain that the conclusion drawn is true?

A. Captain Rick caught his trout in the Little Pony River.
B. There is no size limit on trout mentioned in the law.
C. A trout is a species of fish.
D. None of the above

6. <u>Summary of Evidence Collected to Date</u>: 6.____

I. Some of the doctors in the ICU have been sued for malpractice.
II. Some of the doctors in the ICU are pediatricians.

<u>Prematurely Drawn Conclusion</u>: Some of the pediatricians in the ICU have never been sued for malpractice.

Which of the following pieces of evidence, if any, would make it reasonably certain that the conclusion drawn is true?

A. The number of pediatricians in the ICU is the same as the number of doctors who have been sued for malpractice.
B. The number of pediatricians in the ICU is smaller than the number of doctors who have been sued for malpractice.
C. The number of ICU doctors who have been sued for malpractice is smaller than the number who are pediatricians.
D. None of the above

7. <u>Summary of Evidence Collected to Date</u>: 7.____

I. Along Paseo Boulevard, there are five convenience stores.
II. EZ-GO is east of Pop-a-Shop.
III. Kwik-E-Mart is west of Bob's Market.
IV. The Nightwatch is between EZ-GO and Kwik-E-Mart.

<u>Prematurely Drawn Conclusion</u>: Pop-a-Shop is the westernmost convenience store on Paseo Boulevard.

Which of the following pieces of evidence, if any, would make it reasonably certain that the conclusion drawn is true?

A. Bob's Market is the easternmost convenience store on Paseo.
B. Kwik-E-Mart is the second store from the west.
C. The Nightwatch is west of the EZ-GO.
D. None of the above

8. Summary of Evidence Collected to Date: 8.____
Stark drove home from work at 70 miles an hour and wasn't breaking the law.
Prematurely Drawn Conclusion: Stark was either on an interstate highway or in the state of Montana.
Which of the following pieces of evidence, if any, would make it reasonably certain that the conclusion drawn is true?

A. There are no interstate highways in Montana.
B. Montana is the only state that allows a speed of 70 miles an hour on roads other than interstate highways.
C. Most states don't allow speed of 70 miles an hour on state highways.
D. None of the above

9. Summary of Evidence Collected to Date: 9.____
I. Margaret, owner of MetroWoman magazine, signed a contract with each of her salespeople promising an automatic $200 bonus to any employee who sells more than 60 subscriptions in a calendar month.
II. Lynn sold 82 subscriptions to MetroWoman in the month of December.
Prematurely Drawn Conclusion: Lynn received a $20 bonus.
Which of the following pieces of evidence, if any, would make it reasonably certain that the conclusion is true?

A. Lynn is a salesperson.
B. Lynn works for Margaret.
C. Margaret offered only $200 regardless of the number of subscriptions sold.
D. None of the above

Questions 10-14.

DIRECTIONS: Questions 10 through 14 refer to Map #3 and measure your ability to orient yourself within a given section of town, neighborhood or particular area. Each of the questions describes a starting point and a destination. Assume that you are driving a car in the area shown on the map accompanying the questions. Use the map as a basis for the shortest way to get from one point to another without breaking the law.
On the map, a street marked by arrows, or by arrows and the words "One Way," indicates one-way travel and should be assumed to be one-way for the entire length, even when there are breaks or jogs in the street. EXCEPTION: A street that does not have the same name over the full length.

4 (#1)

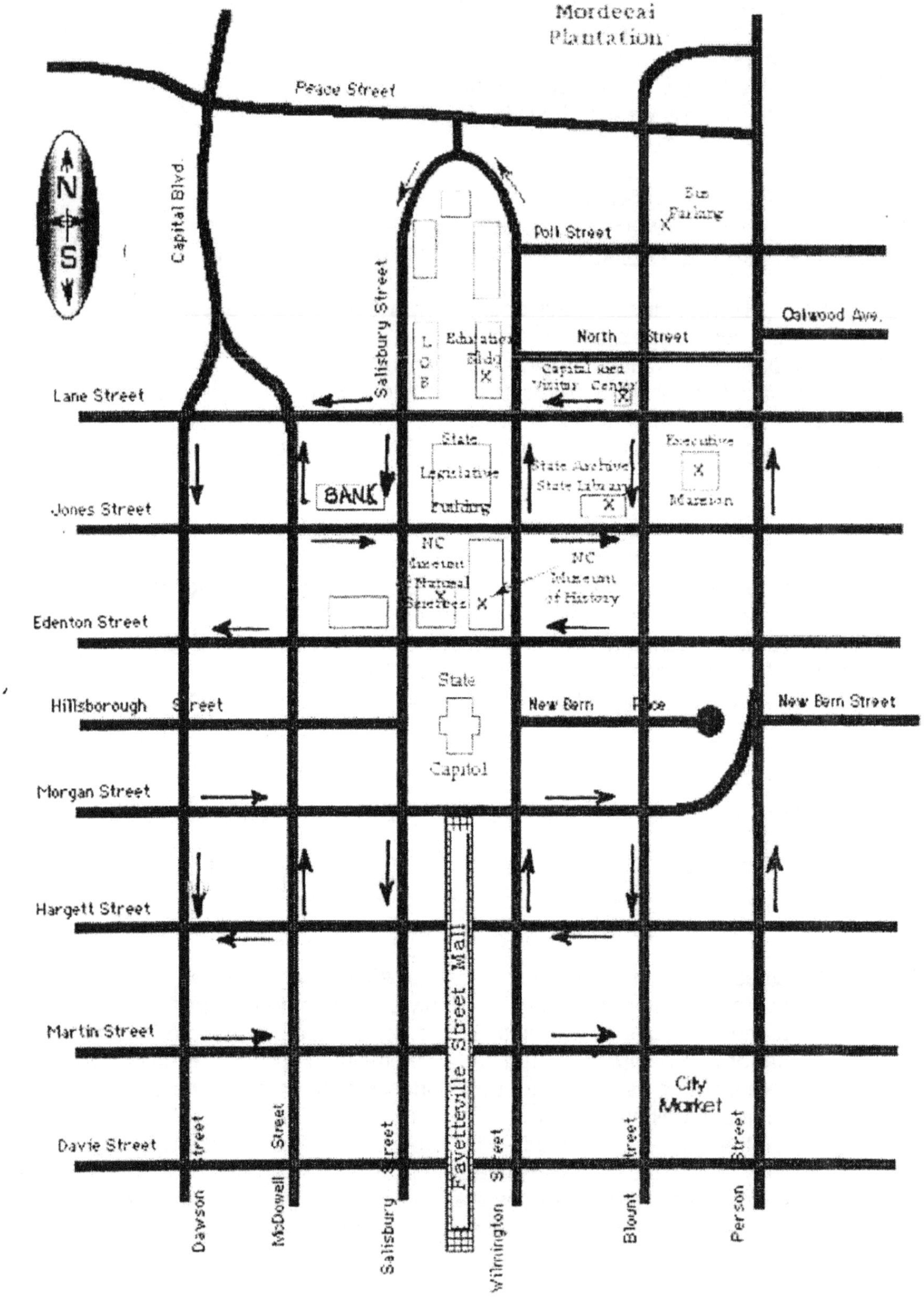

Mordecai Plantation
Peace Street
Capital Blvd.
N
S
Poll Street
Oakwood Ave.
North Street
Salisbury Street
Lane Street
Jones Street
BANK
State Legislative Building
Executive Mansion
Edenton Street
NC Museum of History
Hillsborough
New Bern
New Bern Street
State Capitol
Morgan Street
Hargett Street
Martin Street
City Market
Davie Street
Fayetteville Street Mall
Dawson Street
McDowell Street
Salisbury Street
Wilmington Street
Blount Street
Person Street

10. The SHORTEST legal way from the south end of the Fayetteville Street Mall, at Davie Street, to the city of Raleigh Municipal Building is 10.____
   A. west on Davie, north on McDowell
   B. west on Davie, north on Dawson
   C. east on Davie, north on Wilmington, west on Morgan
   D. east on Davie, north on Wilmington, west on Hargett

11. The SHORTEST legal way from the City Market to the Education Building is 11.____
   A. north on Blount, west on North
   B. north on Person, west on Lane
   C. north on Blount, west on Lane
   D. west on Martin, north on Wilmington

12. The SHORTEST legal way from the Education Building to the State Capitol is 12.____
   A. south on Wilmington
   B. north on Wilmington, west on Peace, south on Capitol, bear west to go south on Dawson, and east on Morgan
   C. west on Lane, south on Salisbury
   D. each on North, south on Blount, west on Edenton

13. The SHORTEST legal way from the State Capitol to Peace College is 13.____
   A. north on Wilmington, jog north, east on Peace
   B. east on Morgan, north on Person, west on Peace
   C. west on Edenton, north on McDowell, north on Capitol Blvd., east on Peace
   D. east on Morgan, north on Blount, west on Peace

14. The SHORTEST legal way from the State Legislative Building to the City Market is 14.____
   A. south on Wilmington, east on Martin
   B. east on Jones, south on Blount
   C. south on Salisbury, east on Davie
   D. east on Lane, south on Blount

Questions 15-19.

DIRECTIONS: Questions 15 through 19 refer to Figure #3, on the following page, and measure your ability to understand written descriptions of events. Each question presents a description of an accident or event and asks you which of the following five drawings in Figure #3 BEST represents it.
In the drawings, the following symbols are used:
Moving vehicle Non-moving vehicle
Pedestrian or bicyclist •
The path and direction of travel of a vehicle or pedestrian is indicated by a solid line.
The path and direction of travel of each vehicle or pedestrian directly involved in a collision from the point of impact is indicated by a dotted line.

6 (#1)

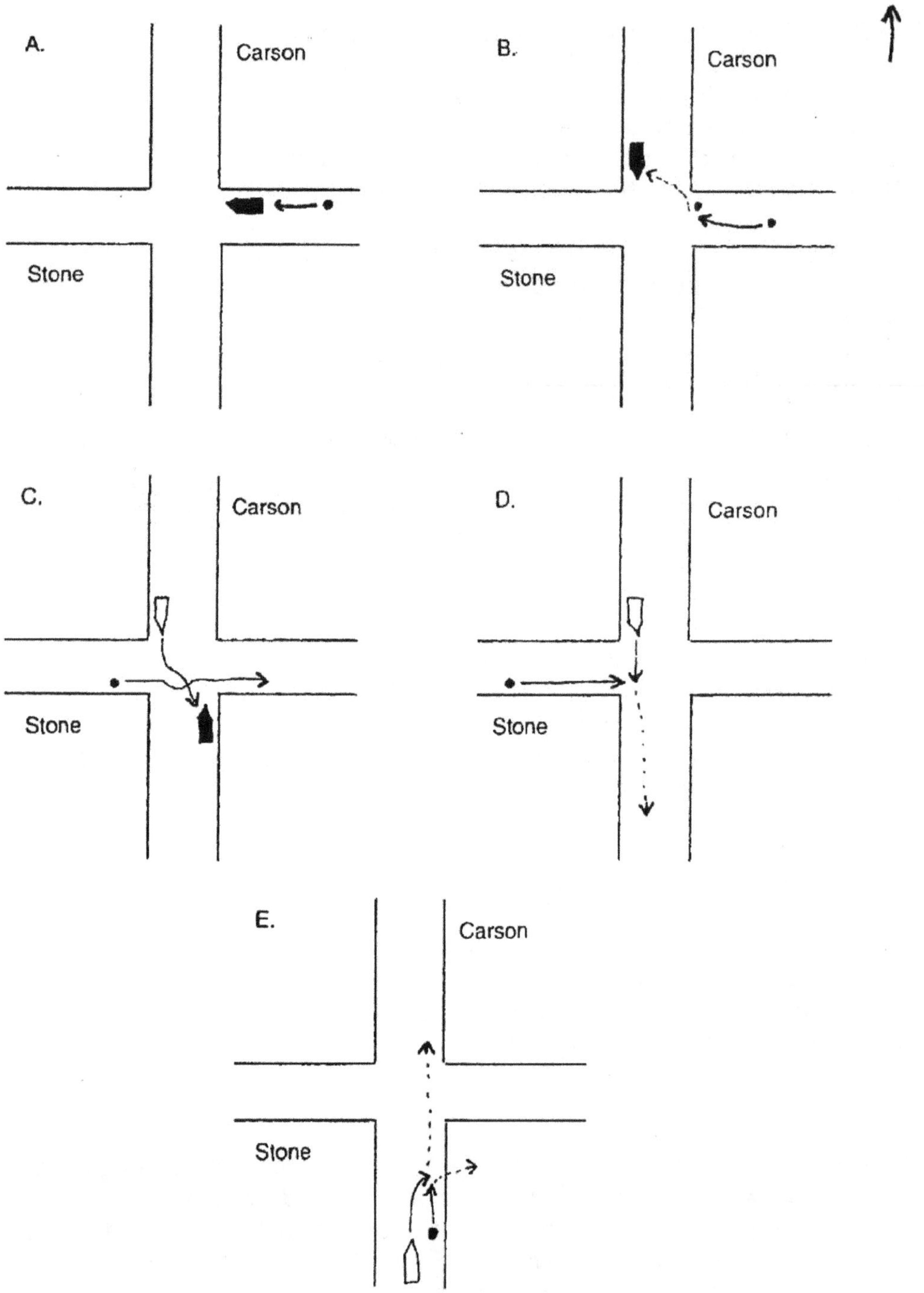


In the space at the right, print the letter of the drawing that BEST fit the descriptions written below.

15. A driver headed north on Carson veers to the right and strikes a bicyclist who is also headed north. The bicyclist is thrown from the road. The driver flees north on Carson. 15.____

16. A driver heading south on Carson runs the stop sign and barely misses colliding with an eastbound cyclist. The cyclist swerves to avoid the collision and continues traveling east. The driver swerves to avoid the collision and strikes a car parked in the northbound lane on Carson. 16.____

17. A bicyclist heading west on Stone collides with a pedestrian in the crosswalk, then veers through the intersection and collides with the front of a car parked in the southbound lane on Carson. 17.____

18. A driver traveling south on Carson runs over a bicyclist who has run the stop sign, and then flees south on Carson. 18.____

19. A bicyclist heading west on Stone collides with the rear of a car parked in the westbound lane. 19.____

Questions 20-22.

DIRECTIONS: In Questions 20 through 22, choose the word or phrase CLOSEST in meaning to the word or phrase printed in capital letters.

20. INSOLVENT 20.____
    A. bankrupt B. vagrant C. hazardous D. illegal

21. TENANT 21.____
    A. laborer B. occupant C. owner D. creditor

22. INFRACTION 22.____
    A. portion B. violation C. remark D. detour

Questions 23-25.

DIRECTIONS: Questions 23 through 25 measure your ability to do fieldwork-related arithmetic. Each question presents a separate arithmetic problem for you to solve.

23. Officer Jones has served on the police force longer than Smith. Smith has served longer than Moore. Moore has served less time than Jones, and Park has served longer than Jones. 23.____
    Which officer has served the LONGEST on the police force?
    A. Jones B. Smith C. Moore D. Park

24. A car wash has raised the price of an outside-only wash from $4 to $5. The car wash applies the same percentage increase to its inside-and-out wash, which was $10. 24.____
    What is the new cost of the inside-and-out wash?
    A. $8 B. $11 C. $12.50 D. $15

25. Ron and James, college students, make $10 an hour working at the restaurant. Ron works 13 hours a week and James works 20 hours a week. 25.____
To make the same amount that Ron earns in a year, James would work about _____ weeks.
A. 18 B. 27 C. 34 D. 45

---

# KEY (CORRECT ANSWERS)

1. C
2. D
3. B
4. B
5. A

6. D
7. B
8. B
9. B
10. A

11. B
12. C
13. A
14. B
15. E

16. C
17. B
18. D
19. A
20. A

21. B
22. B
23. D
24. C
25. C

## SOLUTIONS TO QUESTIONS 1-9

P implies Q = original statement

Not Q implies not P = contrapositive of the original statement. A statement and its contrapositive are logically equivalent.

Q implies P = converse of the original statement

Not P implies not Q = inverse of the original statement. The converse and inverse of an original statement are logically equivalent.

P implies Q = Not P or Q.

1. The CORRECT answer is C.
   Item I is wrong because "some employees" means "at least one employee" and possibly "all employees." If it is true that all employees have fully vested pensions, then the second statement is false. Item II is correct because the second statement is the contrapositive of the first statement.

2. The CORRECT answer is D.
   Item I is wrong because the converse of a statement does not necessarily follow from the original statement. Item II is wrong because statement I implies that there are no Hutchinson family members who live outside Lindsborg.

3. The CORRECT answer is B. Item I is correct because it is composed of the same two compound statements that are simply mentioned in a different order. Item II is correct because if each person is taller than Officer Banks, then there is no person in that precinct who can possibly be shorter than Officer Banks.

4. The CORRECT answer is B.
   Item I is correct because the second statement is the contrapositive of the first statement. Item II is correct because each statement indicates that mowing the hay fields on a particular day leads to the presence of mice the next day.

5. The CORRECT answer is A.
   If Captain Rick caught his trout in the Little Pony River, then we can conclude that he was fishing there. Since statement I says that fishing in the Little Pony Rive is against the law, we conclude that Captain Rick broke the law.

6. The CORRECT answer is D.
   The number of doctors in each group, whether the same or not, has no bearing on the conclusion. There is nothing in evidence to suggest that the group of doctors sued for malpractice overlaps with the group of doctors that are pediatricians.

7. The CORRECT answer is B.
   If we are given that Kwik-E-Mart is the second store from the west, then the order of stores from west to east, is Pop-a-Shop, Kwik-E-Mart, Nightwatch, EZ-GO, and Bob's Market.

8. The CORRECT answer is B.
We are given that Stark drove at 70 miles per hour and didn't break the law. If we also know that Montana is the only state that allows a speed of 70 miles per hour, then we can conclude that Stark must have been driving in Montana or else was driving on some interstate.

9. The CORRECT answer is B.
The only additional piece of information needed is that Lynn works for Margaret. This will guarantee that Lynn receives the promised $200 bonus.

# TEST 2

DIRECTIONS: Each question or incomplete statement is followed by several suggested answers or completions. Select the one that BEST answers the question or completes the statement. *PRINT THE LETTER OF THE CORRECT ANSWER IN THE SPACE AT THE RIGHT.*

Questions 1-9.

DIRECTIONS: Questions 1 through 9 measure your ability to (1) determine whether statements from witnesses say essentially the same thing and (2) determine the evidence needed to make it reasonably certain that a particular conclusion is true.
To do well on this part of the test, you do NOT have to have a working knowledge of police procedures and techniques. Nor do you have to have any more familiarity with criminals and criminal behavior than that acquired from reading newspapers, listening to radio or watching TV. To do well in this part, you must read and reason carefully.

1. Which of the following pairs of statements say essentially the same thing in two different ways? 1.____
   I. All of the teachers at Slater Middle School are intelligent, but some are irrational thinkers.
   Although some teachers at Slater Middle School are irrational thinkers, all of them are intelligent.
   II. Nobody has no friends.
   Everybody has at least one friend.
   The CORRECT answer is:
   A. I only B. I and II C. II only D. Neither I nor II

2. Which of the following pairs of statements say essentially the same thing in two different ways? 2.____
   I. Although bananas taste good to most people, they are also a healthy food.
   Bananas are a healthy food, but most people eat them because they taste good.
   II. If Dr. Jones is in, we should call at the office.
   Either Dr. Jones is in, or we should not call at the office.
   The CORRECT answer is:
   A. I only B. I and II C. II only D. Neither I nor II

3 Which of the following pairs of statements say essentially the same thing in two different ways? 3.____
   I. Some millworker work two shifts.
   If someone works only one shift, he is probably not a millworker.
   II. If a letter carrier clocks in at nine, he can finish his route by the end of the day.
   If a letter carrier does not clock in at nine, he cannot finish his route by the end of the day.
   The CORRECT answer is:
   A. I only B. I and II C. II only D. Neither I nor II

4. Which of the following pairs of statements say essentially the same thing in two different ways? 4.____
   I. If a member of the swim team attends every practice, he will compete in the next meet.
      Either a swim team member will compete in the next meet, or he did not attend every practice.
   II. All the engineers in the drafting department who wear glasses know how to use AutoCAD.
      If an engineer wears glasses, he will know how to use AutoCAD.

   The CORRECT answer is:
   A. I only B. I and II C. II only D. Neither I nor II

5. <u>Summary of Evidence Collected to Date</u>: 5.____
   All of the parents who attend the weekly parenting seminars are high school graduates.
   <u>Prematurely Drawn Conclusion</u>: Some parents who attend the weekly parenting seminars have been convicted of child abuse.
   Which of the following pieces of evidence, if any, would make it reasonably certain that the conclusion drawn is true?
   A. Those convicted of child abuse are often high school graduates.
   B. Some high school graduates have been convicted of child abuse.
   C. There is no correlation between education level and the incidence of child abuse.
   D. None of the above

6. <u>Summary of Evidence Collected to Date</u>: 6.____
   I. Mr. Cantwell promised to vote for new school buses if he was reelected to the board.
   II. If the new school buses are approved by the school board, then Mr. Cantwell was not reelected to the board.

   <u>Prematurely Drawn Conclusion</u>: Approval of the new school buses was defeated in spite of Mr. Cantwell's vote.
   Which of the following pieces of evidence, if any, would make it reasonably certain that the conclusion drawn is true?
   A. Mr. Cantwell decided not to run for reelection.
   B. Mr. Cantwell was reelected to the board.
   C. Mr. Cantwell changed his mind and voted against the new buses.
   D. None of the above

7. <u>Summary of Evidence Collected to Date</u>: 7.____
   I. The station employs three detectives: Francis, Jackson, and Stern. One of the detectives is a lieutenant, one is a sergeant, and one is a major.
   II. Francis is not a lieutenant.

   <u>Prematurely Drawn Conclusion</u>: Jackson is a lieutenant.
   Which of the following pieces of evidence, if any, would make it reasonably certain that the conclusion drawn is true?
   A. Stern is not a sergeant. B. Stern is a major.
   C. Francis is a major. E. None of the above

8. Summary of Evidence Collected to Date: 8.____
I. In the office building, every survival kit that contains a gas mask also contains anthrax vaccine.
II. Some of the kits containing water purification tablets also contain anthrax vaccine.
Prematurely Drawn Conclusion: If the survival kit near the typists' pool contains a gas mask, it does not contain water purification tablets.
Which of the following pieces of evidence, if any, would make it reasonably certain that the conclusion drawn is true?
A. Some survival kits contain all three items.
B. The survival kit near the typists' pool contains anthrax vaccine.
C. The survival kit near the typists' pool contains only two of these items.
D. None of the above

9. Summary of Evidence Collected to Date: 9.____
The shrink-wrap mechanism is designed to shut itself off if the heating coil temperature drops below 400 during the twin cycle.
Prematurely Drawn Conclusion: If the machine was operating the twin cycle on Monday, it was not operating properly.
Which of the following pieces of evidence, if any, would make it reasonably certain that the conclusion drawn is true?
A. On Monday, the heating coil temperature reached 450.
B. When the machine performs functions other than the twin cycle, the heating coil temperature sometimes drops below 400.
C. The shrink-wrap mechanism did not shut itself off on Monday.
D. None of the above

Questions 10-14.

DIRECTIONS: Questions 10 through 14 refer to Map #3 and measure your ability to orient yourself within a given section of town, neighborhood or particular area. Each of the questions describes a starting point and a destination. Assume that you are driving a car in the area shown on the map accompanying the questions. Use the map as a basis for the shortest way to get from one point to another without breaking the law.
On the map, a street marked by arrows, or by arrows and the words "One Way," indicates one-way travel and should be assumed to be one-way for the entire length, even when there are breaks or jogs in the street. EXCEPTION: A street that does not have the same name over the full length.

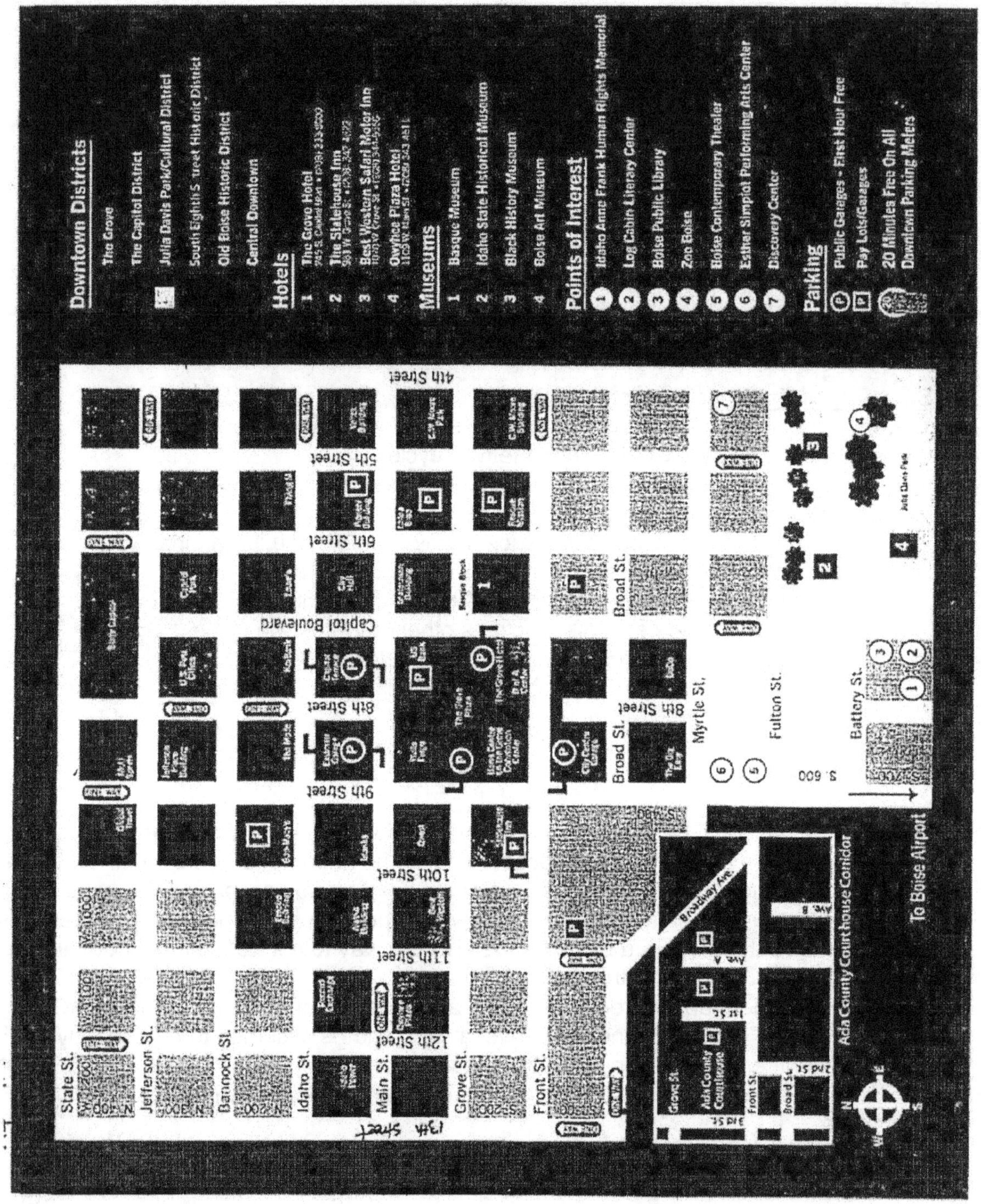


10. The SHORTEST legal way from the State Capitol to Idaho Power is  10.____
   A. south on Capitol Blvd., west on Main, north on 12th
   B. south on 8th, west on Main
   C. west on Jefferson, south on 12th
   D. south on Capitol Blvd., west on Front, north on 12th

11. The SHORTEST legal way from the Jefferson Place Building to the Statesman Building is 11.____
    A. east on Jefferson, south on Capitol Blvd.
    B. south on 8th, east on Main
    C. east on Jefferson, south on 4th, west on Main
    D. south on 9th, east on Main

12. The SHORTEST legal way from Julia Davis Park to Owyhee Plaza Hotel is 12.____
    A. north on 5th, west on Front, north on 11th
    B. north on 6th, west on Main
    C. west on Battery, north on 9th, west on Front, north on Main
    D. north on 5th, west on Front, north on 13th, east on Main

13. The SHORTEST legal way from the Big Easy to City Hall is 13.____
    A. north on 9th, east on Main
    B. east on Myrtle, north on Capitol Blvd.
    C. north on 9th, east on Idaho
    D. east on Myrtle, north on 6th

14. The SHORTEST legal way from the Boise Contemporary Theater to the Pioneer Building is 14.____
    A. north on 9th, east on Main
    B. north on 9th, east on Myrtle, north on 6th
    C. east on Fulton, north on Capitol Blvd., east on Main
    D. east on Fulton, north on 6th

Questions 15-19.

DIRECTIONS: Questions 15 through 19 refer to Figure #3, on the following page, and measure your ability to understand written descriptions of events. Each question presents a description of an accident or event and asks you which of the following five drawings in Figure #3 BEST represents it.
In the drawings, the following symbols are used:
Moving vehicle  Non-moving vehicle 
Pedestrian or bicyclist •
The path and direction of travel of a vehicle or pedestrian is indicated by a solid line.
The path and direction of travel of each vehicle or pedestrian directly involved in a collision from the point of impact is indicated by a dotted line.

In the space at the right, print the letter of the drawing that BEST fit the descriptions written below.

A.

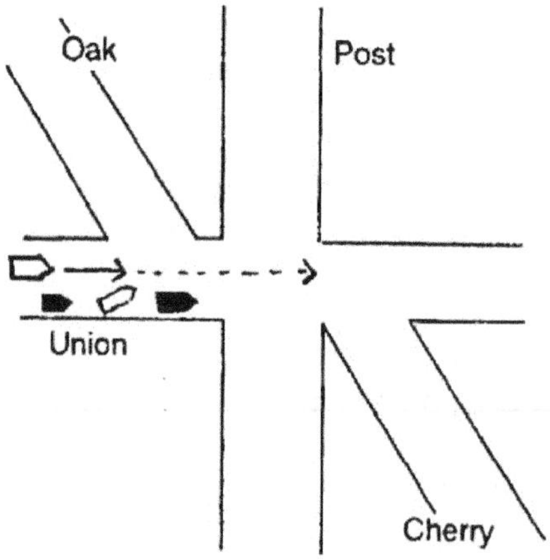
Oak
Post
Union
Cherry

B.

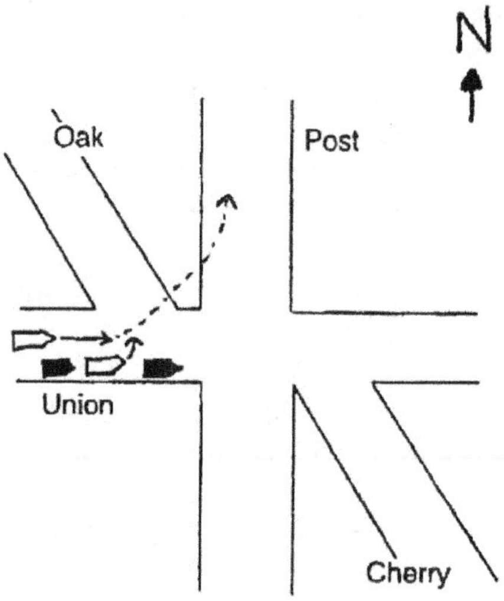
N
Oak
Post
Union
Cherry

C.

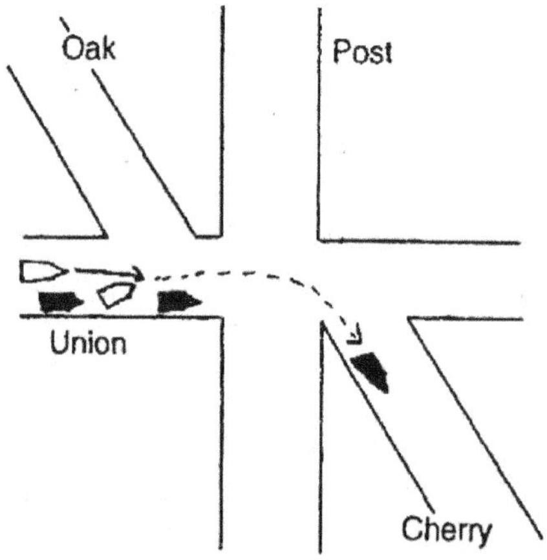
Oak
Post
Union
Cherry

D.

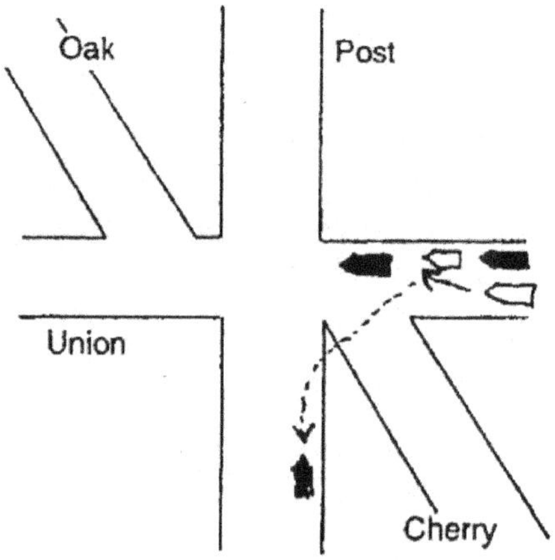
Oak
Post
Union
Cherry

E.

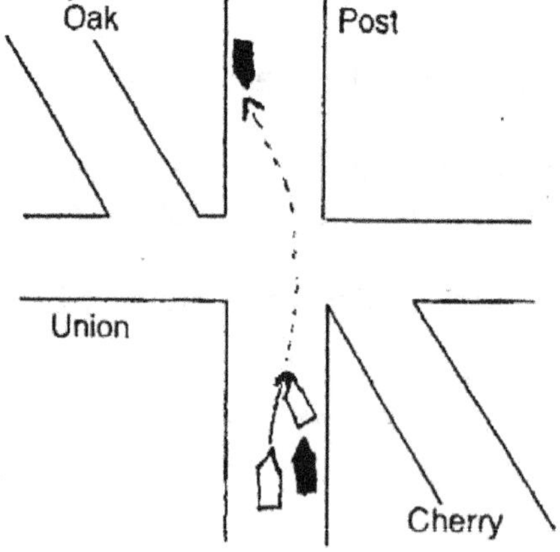
Oak
Post
Union
Cherry

15. A driver headed east on Union strikes a car that is pulling out from between two parked cars, and then continues east. 15.____

16. A driver headed north on Post strikes a car that is pulling out from in front of a parked car, then veers into the oncoming lane and collides head-on with a car that is parked in the southbound lane of Post. 16.____

17. A driver headed east on Union strikes a car that is pulling out from two parked cars, travels through the intersection, and makes a sudden right turn onto Cherry, where he strikes a parked car in the rear. 17.____

18. A driver headed west on Union strikes a car that is pulling out from between two parked cars, and then swerves to the left. He cuts the corner and travels over the sidewalk at the intersection of Cherry and Post, and then strikes a car that is parked in the northbound lane on Post. 18.____

19. A driver headed east on Union strikes a car that is pulling out from between two parked cars, and then swerves to the left. He cuts the corner and travels over the sidewalk at the intersection of Oak and Post, and then flees north on Post. 19.____

Questions 20-22.

DIRECTIONS: In Questions 20 through 22, choose the word or phrase CLOSEST in meaning to the word or phrase printed in capital letters.

20. TITLE 20.____
A. danger B. ownership C. description D. treatise

21. REVOKE 21.____
A. cancel B. imagine C. solicit D. cause

22. BRIEF 22.____
A. summary B. ruling C. plea D. motion

Questions 23-25.

DIRECTIONS: Questions 23 through 25 measure your ability to do fieldwork-related arithmetic. Each question presents a separate arithmetic problem for you to solve.

23. An investigator plans to drive from his home to Los Angeles, a trip of 2,800 miles. His car has a 24-gallon tank and gets 18 miles to the gallon. 23.____
If he starts out with a full tank of gasoline, what is the FEWEST number of stops he will have to make for gasoline to complete his trip to Los Angeles?
A. 4 B. 5 C. 6 D. 7

24. A caseworker has 24 home visits to schedule for a week. She will visit three homes on Sunday, and on every day that follows she will visit one more home than she visited on the previous day. 24.____
At the end of the day on _____, the caseworker will have completed all of her home visits.
   A. Wednesday   B. Thursday   C. Friday   D. Saturday

25. Ms. Langhorn takes a cab from her house to the airport. The cab company charges $3.00 to start the meter and $.50 per mile after that. It's 15 miles from Ms. Langhorn's house to the airport. 25.____
How much will she have to pay for a cab?
   A. $10.50   B. $11.50   C. $14.00   D. $15.50

---

## KEY (CORRECT ANSWERS)

| | | | |
|---|---|---|---|
| 1. | B | 11. | D |
| 2. | A | 12. | A |
| 3. | D | 13. | B |
| 4. | B | 14. | C |
| 5. | D | 15. | A |
| 6. | B | 16. | E |
| 7. | B | 17. | C |
| 8. | C | 18. | D |
| 9. | C | 19. | B |
| 10. | C | 20. | B |

| | |
|---|---|
| 21. | A |
| 22. | A |
| 23. | C |
| 24. | B |
| 25. | A |

## SOLUTIONS TO QUESTIONS 1-9

P implies Q = original statement

Not Q implies not P = contrapositive of the original statement. A statement and its contrapositive are logically equivalent.

Q implies P = converse of the original statement

Not P implies not Q = inverse of the original statement. The converse and inverse of an original statement are logically equivalent.

P implies Q = Not P or Q.

1. The CORRECT answer is B.
   For Item I, the irrational thinking teachers at the Middle School belong the group of all Middle School teachers. Since all teachers at the Middle School are intelligent, this includes the subset of irrational thinkers. For item II, if no one person has no friends, this implies that each person must have at least one friend.

2. The CORRECT answer is A.
   In item I, both statements state that (a) bananas are healthy and (b) bananas are eaten mainly because they taste good. In item II, the second statement is not equivalent to the first statement. An equivalent statement to the first statement would be "Either Dr. Jones is not in or we should call at the office."

3. The CORRECT answer is D.
   In item I, given that a person works one shift, we cannot draw any conclusion about whether he/she is a millworker. It is possible that a millworker works one, two, or a number more than two shifts. In item II, the second statement is the inverse of the first statement; they are not logically equivalent.

4. The CORRECT answer is B.
   In item I, any statement in the form "P implies Q" is equivalent to "Not P or Q." In this case, P = A member of the swim team attends practice, and Q = He will compete in the next meet. In item II, "P implies Q" is equivalent to "all P belongs to Q." In this case, P = Engineer wears glasses, and Q = He will know how to use AutoCAD.

5. The CORRECT answer is D. Because the number of high school graduates is so much larger than the number of convicted child abusers, none of the additional pieces of evidence make it reasonably certain that there are convicted abusers within this group of parents.

6. The CORRECT answer is B.
   Statement II is equivalent to "If Mr. Cantwell is reelected to the school board, then school buses are not approved. Statement I assures us that Mr. Cantwell will vote for new school buses. The only logical conclusion is that in spite of Mr. Cantwell's reelection to the board and subsequent vote, approval of the buses was still defeated.

7. The CORRECT answer is B. From Statement II, we conclude that Francis is either a sergeant or a major. If we also know that Stern is a major, we can deduce that Francis is a sergeant. This means that the third person, Jackson, must be a lieutenant.

8. The CORRECT answer is C.
Given that a survival kit contains a gas mask, Statement I assures us that it also contains the anthrax vaccine. If the survival kit near the typist pool only contains two items, than we can conclude that the gas mask in this location cannot contain a third item, namely the anthrax vaccine.

9. The CORRECT answer is C.
The original statement can be written in "P implies Q" form, where P = the heating coil temperature drops below 400 during the twin cycle, and Q = the mechanism shuts itself off. The contrapositive (which must be true) would be "If the mechanism did not shut itself off then the heating coil temperature did not drop below 400." We would then conclude that the temperature was too high and, therefore, the machine did not operate properly.

# INTERVIEWING
# EXAMINATION SECTION
# TEST 1

DIRECTIONS: Each question or incomplete statement is followed by several suggested answers or completions. Select the one that BEST answers the question or completes the statement. *PRINT THE LETTER OF THE CORRECT ANSWER IN THE SPACE AT THE RIGHT.*

1. Of the following, the BEST way for an interviewer to calm a person who seems to have become emotionally upset as a result of a question asked is for the interviewer to 1.____

   A. talk to the person about other things for a short time
   B. ask that the person control himself
   C. probe for the cause of his emotional upset
   D. finish the questioning as quickly as possible

2. You find that an applicant is hesitant about showing you some required personal material and documents. Your *initial* reaction to this situation should be to 2.____

   A. quietly insist that he give you the required materials
   B. make an exception in his case to avoid making him uncomfortable
   C. suspect that he may be trying to withhold evidence
   D. understand that he is in a stressful situation and may feel ashamed to reveal such information

3. An applicant has just given you a response which does not seem clear. 3.____
   Of the following, the BEST course of action for you to take in order to check your understanding of the applicant's response is for you to

   A. ask the question again during a subsequent interview with this applicant
   B. repeat the applicant's answer in the applicant's own words and ask if that is what the applicant meant
   C. later in the interview, repeat the question that led to this response
   D. repeat the question that led to this response, but say it more forcefully

4. While speaking with applicants, you may find that there are times when an applicant will be silent for a short while before answering questions. 4.____
   In order to gather the best information from the applicant, the interviewer should *generally* treat these silences by

   A. repeating the same question to make the applicant stop hesitating
   B. rephrasing the question in a way that the applicant can answer it faster
   C. directing an easier question to the applicant so that he can gain confidence in answering
   D. waiting patiently and not pressuring the applicant into quick, undeveloped answers

5. In dealing with members of *different* ethnic and religious groups among the applicants you interview, you should give 5.____

   A. individuals the services to which they are entitled
   B. less service to those you judge to be more advantaged

C. better service to groups with which you sympathize most
D. better service to groups with political "muscle"

6. You must be sure that, when interviewing an applicant, you phrase each question carefully. 6.____
Of the following, the MOST important reason for this is to insure that

A. the applicant will phrase each of his responses carefully
B. you use correct grammar
C. it is clear to the applicant what information you are seeking
D. you do not word the same question differently for different applicants

7. When given a form to complete, a client hesitates, tells you that he cannot fill out forms too well and that he is afraid he will do a poor job. He asks you to do it for him. You are quite sure, however, that he is able to do it himself. 7.____
In this case, it would be MOST advisable for you to

A. encourage him to try filling out the application as well as he can
B. fill out the application for him
C. explain to him that he must learn to accept responsibility
D. tell him that, if others can fill out an application, he can too

8. Assume that an applicant whom you are interviewing has made a statement that is obviously not true. 8.____
Of the following, the BEST course of action for you to take at this point in the interview is to

A. ask the applicant if he is sure about his statement
B. tell the applicant that his statement is incorrect
C. question the applicant further to clarify his response
D. assume that the statement is correct

9. Assume that you are conducting an *initial* interview with an applicant. 9.____
Of the following, the MOST advisable questions for you to ask at the beginning of this interview are those that

A. can be answered in one or two sentences
B. have nothing to do with the subject matter of the interview
C. are most likely to reveal any hostility on the part of the applicant
D. the applicant is most likely to be willing and able to answer

10. When interviewing a particularly nervous and upset applicant, the one of the following actions which you should take FIRST is to 10.____

A. inform the applicant that, to be helped, he must cooperate
B. advise the applicant that proof must be provided for statements he makes
C. assure the applicant that every effort will be made to provide him with whatever assistance he is entitled to
D. tell the applicant he will have no trouble so long as he is truthful

11. Assume that it is part of your job to prepare a monthly report for your unit head that eventually goes to the director. The report contains information on the number of applicants you have interviewed that have been approved and the number of applicants you have interviewed that have been turned down. Errors on such reports are *serious* because 11.____

A. you are expected to be able to prove how many applicants you have interviewed each month
B. accurate statistics are needed for effective management of the department
C. they may not be discovered before the report is transmitted to the director
D. they may result in a loss to the applicants left out of the report

12. During interviews, people give information about themselves in several ways. 12.____
Which of the following *usually* gives the LEAST amount of information about the person being questioned? His

A. spoken words
B. tone of voice
C. facial expression
D. body position

13. Suppose an applicant, while being interviewed, becomes angered by your questioning and begins to use sharp, uncontrolled language. 13.____
Which of the following is the BEST way for you to react to him?

A. Speak in his style to show him that you are neither impressed nor upset by his speech
B. Interrupt him and tell him that you are not required to listen to this kind of speech
C. Lower your voice and slow the rate of your speech in an attempt to set an example that will calm him
D. Let him continue in his way but insist that he answer your questions directly

14. You have been informed that no determination has yet been made on the eligibility of an applicant whom you have interviewed. The decision depends on further checking. His situation, however, is similar to that of many other applicants whose eligibility has been approved. The applicant, *quite worried,* calls you, and asks whether his application has been accepted. 14.____
What would be BEST for you to do under these circumstances? Tell him

A. his application is being checked and you will let him know the final result as soon as possible
B. that a written request addressed to your supervisor will probably get faster action for his case
C. not to worry since other applicants with similar backgrounds have already been accepted
D. since there is no definite information and you are very busy, you will call him back

15. Suppose that you have been talking with an applicant. You have the feeling from the latest things the applicant has said that some of his answers to earlier questions were not totally correct. You guess that he might have been afraid or confused earlier but that your conversation has now put him in a more comfortable frame of mind. 15.____
In order to test the reliability of information received from the earlier questions, the BEST thing for you to do *now* is to ask new questions that

A. allow the applicant to explain why he deliberately gave false information to you
B. ask for the same information, although worded differently from the original questions
C. put pressure on the applicant so that he personally wants to clear up the facts in his earlier answers
D. indicate to the applicant that you are aware of his deceptiveness

16. While providing you with required information, an applicant whom you are interviewing, informs you that she does not know certain facts.
Of the following, the MOST advisable action for you to take is to 16.____

A. ask her to explain further
B. advise her about research facilities
C. express your sympathy for the situation
D. go on to the next item of information

17. If, in an interview, you wish to determine a client's usual occupation, which one of the following questions is MOST likely to elicit the *most* useful information? 17.____

A. Did you ever work in a factory?
B. Do you know how to do office work?
C. What kind of work do you do?
D. Where are you working now?

18. Assume that you are approached by a clerk from another office who starts questioning you about one of the clients you have just interviewed. The clerk says that she is a relative of the client. According to departmental policy, all matters discussed with clients are to be kept confidential.
Of the following, the BEST course of action for you to take in this situation would be to 18.____

A. check to see whether the clerk is really a relative before you make any further decisions
B. explain to the clerk why you cannot divulge the information
C. tell the clerk that you do not know the answers to her questions
D. tell the clerk that she can get from the client any information the client wishes to give

19. Which of the following is usually the BEST technique for you, as an interviewer, to use to bring an applicant back to subject matter from which the applicant has strayed? 19.____

A. Ask the applicant a question that is related to the subject of the interview
B. Show the applicant that his response is unrelated to the question
C. Discreetly reind the applicant that there is a time allotment for the interview
D. Tell the applicant that you will be happy to discuss the extraneous matters at a future interview

20. Assume that you are interviewing a witness who is telling a story crucial to your investigation. It is important that you get all the facts being related by this witness. In order to secure this vital information, the BEST of the following techniques is to 20.____

A. quietly interrupt the witness's story and request him to speak with deliberation so that you can record his statement
B. guide the witness during his recital so that all important points are validated

C. confine your activities during the story to brief note-taking, and, after the information has been secured, request a full written statement
D. inform the witness that he must relate all the facts as truthfully and concisely as possible

21. The statement of any witness obtained in an interview should GENERALLY be considered 21.____

A. as a lead requiring substantiation by additional evidence
B. accurate if the witness appears honest and is cooperative
C. unreliable if the witness has been involved in similar investigations
D. as a fact admissible under the rules of evidence

22. During an important interview, an interviewer takes notes from time to time but very rarely looks at the subject being questioned. 22.____
Such action on the part of the interviewer is

A. *unacceptable,* chiefly because during the actual interview an interviewer should pay more attention to the witness's manner of giving the information rather than to the content of his statements
B. *acceptable,* chiefly because data should be recorded at the earliest opportunity and important data should be noted meticulously
C. *unacceptable,* chiefly because it inhibits the person being interviewed and is not conducive to a give-and-take discussion
D. *unacceptable,* chiefly because focusing attention on note-taking and not on the person being interviewed creates an impression of professional objectivity

23. Since he must interview persons with various personalities and attitudes, an interviewer should, *generally,* adopt a method of interviewing that 23.____

A. is uniformly applicable to all types so that discrepancies in the accounts of individuals may be readily detected
B. can be adjusted to the persons whom he interviews
C. is based on the premise that most interviewees tend to be uncooperative
D. requires the interviewer to spend as little time as possible in questioning applicants

24. One of the more difficult tasks facing an interviewer is to control the tendency of witnesses to ramble when giving information. 24.____
Of the following, the BEST technique for keeping a witness's comments pertinent is to

A. ask questions which indicate the desired answer
B. insist on "yes" and "no" answers to his questions
C. construct questions that restrict the range of information which the witness can give in response
D. ask precise questions so that the answers of the witness will necessarily be brief

25. During interviews, a certain interviewer phrases follow-up questions mentally during pauses while the subject is still answering the previous question. This practice is, *generally,* 25.____

A. *desirable,* chiefly because it gives the impression that the interviewer is well acquainted with all the facts
B. *undesirable,* chiefly because the interviewer cannot know whether such questions will be appropriate
C. *desirable,* chiefly because it enables the interviewer to pose new questions without significant breaks in the discussion
D. *undesirable,* chiefly because it subjects the person being interviewed to a barrage of questions

# KEY (CORRECT ANSWERS)

1. A
2. D
3. B
4. D
5. A
6. C
7. A
8. C
9. D
10. C
11. B
12. D
13. C
14. A
15. B
16. D
17. C
18. B
19. A
20. C
21. A
22. C
23. B
24. C
25. C

# TEST 2

DIRECTIONS: Each question or incomplete statement is followed by several suggested answers or completions. Select the one that BEST answers the question or completes the statement. *PRINT THE LETTER OF THE CORRECT ANSWER IN THE SPACE AT THE RIGHT.*

1. The one of the following which is the BEST description of a *properly* objective interviewer is one who 1.____

   A. is friendly and sensitive to the client's feelings, without becoming emotionally involved
   B. is distant and impersonal, remaining unaffected by what the client says
   C. lets personal emotions enter as far as the client's situation calls for them
   D. becomes emotionally involved with the client's situation, but without showing this involvement

2. The one of the following which is MOST necessary for successfully intefviewing a person who belongs to a culture different from that of the interviewer is for the interviewer to 2.____

   A. have some appreciation of the other culture
   B. ignore those cultural differences which lead to bias
   C. stay away from sensitive, "touchy" issues
   D. assume the mannerisms of people in the other culture

3. In fact-finding interviews, it is generally assumed that the smaller the lumber of interviewees, the greater the increase of reliability with the addition of others. 3.____
   The PROPER number of interviewees needed to insure the accuracy of information obtained *generally* depends upon the

   A. educational level of those interviewed
   B. number of people who have the required information
   C. directness of the questions asked
   D. variability of the information received

4. The one of the following which is generally MOST likely to be *accurately* described in an interview by an interviewee is 4.____

   A. the presence of a large painting in the interviewer's office
   B. the number of people in the interviewer's waiting room
   C. space relations
   D. duration of time

5. The one of the following which is *generally* the BEST course of action for an interviewer to take when interviewing a person who is reluctant to tell what he knows about a matter under investigation is to 5.____

   A. be curt and abrupt, and threaten the person with the consequences of his withholding information
   B. be firm and severe, and pressure the person into telling the needed information

C. be patient and candid with the person being questioned about the investigation since doing otherwise is not ethical
D. give the person false information about the investigation so he will give the needed information without realizing its importance

6. It is often recommended that an interviewer prepare in advance a list of questions or topics to be covered in an interview. 6.____
The MAIN reason for using such a checklist is to

A. allow investigations to be assigned to less efficient interviewers
B. eliminate a large amount of follow-up paper work
C. aid the interviewer in remembering to cover all important topics
D. aid the interviewer in maintaining an objective distance from the person interviewed

7. *Usually,* the CHIEF advantage of a directive approach in an interview is that the 7.____

A. interviewer maintains control over the course of the interview
B. person interviewed is more likely to be put at ease
C. person interviewed is generally left free to direct the interview
D. interviewer will not suggest answers to the person interviewed

8. *Usually,* the CHIEF advantage of a non-directive approach in conducting an interview is that the 8.____

A. interviewer generally conceals what he is looking for in the interview
B. person interviewed is more likely to express his true feelings about the topic under discussion
C. person interviewed is more likely to follow an idea introduced by the interviewer
D. interviewer can keep the discussion limited to topics he believes to be relevant

9. The one of the following which is generally the LEAST likely to be *accurate* in a description of an event given to an interviewer is a statement about 9.____

A. the presence of an object
B. the number of people, when their number is small
C. locations of people
D. duration of time

10. Assume that you, an interviewer, are conducting a character investigation. 10.____
In an interview, the one of the following character traits of the person being interviewed which can *usually* be determined with a GOOD degree of reliability is

A. honesty
B. dependability
C. forcefulness
D. perseverance

11. You have been assigned the task of obtaining a family's social history. 11.____
The BEST place for you to interview members of the family while obtaining this social history would, *generally,* be in

A. the family's home
B. your agency's general offices
C. the home of a friend of the family
D. your own private office

12. If an interviewer obtains testimony from persons in interviews by means of interrogation or asking questions rather than by letting the person freely relate the testimony, what is said will, *generally,* be 12.____

    A. *greater* in range and *less* accurate
    B. *greater* in range and *more* accurate
    C. about the *same* in range and *less* accurate
    D. about the *same* in range and *more* accurate

13. Experienced interviewers have learned to phrase their questions carefully in order to obtain the desired response. Of the following, the question which would *usually* elicit the MOST accurate answer is: 13.____

    A. "How old are you?"
    B. "What is your income?"
    C. "How are you today?"
    D. "What is your date of birth?"

14. The one of the following questions which would *generally* lead to the LEAST reliable answer is: 14.____

    A. "Did you see a wallet?"
    B. "Was the German Shepherd gray?"
    C. "Didn't you see the stop sign?"
    D. "Did you see the guard on duty?"

15. Some interviewers may make a practice of observing details of the surroundings when interviewing in someone's home or office. Such a practice is, *generally,* considered 15.____

    A. *undesirable,* mainly because such snooping is an unwarranted, unethical invasion of privacy
    B. *undesirable,* mainly because useful information is rarely, if ever, gained this way
    C. *desirable,* mainly because useful insights into the character of the person interviewed may be gained
    D. *desirable,* mainly because it is impossible to evaluate a person adequately without such observation of his environment

# KEY (CORRECT ANSWERS)

| | | | | | |
|---|---|---|---|---|---|
| 1. | A | 6. | C | 11. | A |
| 2. | A | 7. | A | 12. | A |
| 3. | D | 8. | B | 13. | D |
| 4. | A | 9. | D | 14. | B |
| 5. | C | 10. | C | 15. | C |

# PREPARING WRITTEN MATERIAL

## PARAGRAPH REARRANGEMENT COMMENTARY

The sentences that follow are in scrambled order. You are to rearrange them in proper order and indicate the letter choice containing the correct answer at the space at the right.

Each group of sentences in this section is actually a paragraph presented in scrambled order. Each sentence in the group has a place in that paragraph; no sentence is to be left out. You are to read each group of sentences and decide upon the best order in which to put the sentences so as to form a well-organized paragraph.

The questions in this section measure the ability to solve a problem when all the facts relevant to its solution are not given.

More specifically, certain positions of responsibility and authority require the employee to discover connection between events sometimes, apparently, unrelated. In order to do this, the employee will find it necessary to correctly infer that unspecified events have probably occurred or are likely to occur. This ability becomes especially important when action must be taken on incomplete information.

Accordingly, these questions require competitors to choose among several suggested alternatives, each of which presents a different sequential arrangement of the events. Competitors must choose the MOST logical of the suggested sequences.

In order to do so, they may be required to draw on general knowledge to infer missing concepts or events that are essential to sequencing the given events. Competitors should be careful to infer only what is essential to the sequence. The plausibility of the wrong alternatives will always require the inclusion of unlikely events or of additional chains of events which are NOT essential to sequencing the given events.

It's very important to remember that you are looking for the best of the four possible choices, and that the best choice of all may not even be one of the answers you're given to choose from.

There is no one right way to solve these problems. Many people have found it helpful to first write out the order of the sentences, as they would have arranged them, on their scrap paper before looking at the possible answers. If their optimum answer is there, this can save them some time. If it isn't, this method can still give insight into solving the problem. Others find it most helpful to just go through each of the possible choices, contrasting each as they go along. You should use whatever method feels comfortable and works for you.

While most of these types of questions are not that difficult, we've added a higher percentage of the difficult type, just to give you more practice. Usually there are only one or two questions on this section that contain such subtle distinctions that you're unable to answer confidently. And you then may find yourself stuck deciding between two possible choices, neither of which you're sure about.

---

# EXAMINATION SECTION

## TEST 1

DIRECTIONS: The sentences that follow are in scrambled order. You are to rearrange them in proper order and indicate the letter choice containing the correct answer. *PRINT THE LETTER OF THE CORRECT ANSWER IN THE SPACE AT THE RIGHT.*

1. Below are four statements labeled W, X, Y and Z. 1.____
   W. He was a strict and fanatic drillmaster.
   X. The word is always used in a derogatory sense and generally shows resentment and anger on the part of the user.
   Y. It is from the name of this Frenchman that we derive our English word, martinet.
   Z. Jean Martinet was the Inspector-General of Infantry during the reign of King Louis XIV.
   The PROPER order in which these sentences should be placed in a paragraph is:
   A. X, Z, W, Y  B. X, Z, Y, W  C. Z, W, Y, X  D. Z, Y, W, X

2. In the following paragraph, the sentences, which are numbered, have been jumbled. 2.____
   I. Since then it has undergone changes.
   II. It was incorporated in 1955 under the laws of the State of New York.
   III. Its primary purposes, a cleaner city, has, however, remained the same.
   IV. The Citizens Committee works in cooperation with the Mayor's Inter-departmental Committee for a Clean City. 3.____
   The order in which these sentences should be arranged to form a well-organized paragraph is:
   A. II, IV, I, III  B. III, IV, I, II  C. IV, II, I, III  D. IV, III, II, I

Questions 3-5.

DIRECTIONS: The sentences listed below are part of a meaningful paragraph but they are not given in their proper order. You are to decide what would be the BEST order in which to put the sentences so as to form a well-organized paragraph. Each sentence has a place in the paragraph; there are no extra sentences. You are then to answer Questions 3 through 5 inclusive on the basis of your rearrangements of these scrambled sentences into a properly organized paragraph.

In 1887 some insurance companies organized an Inspection Department to advise their clients on all phases of fire prevention and protection. Probably this has been due to the smaller annual fire losses in Great Britain than in the United States. It tests various fire prevention devices and appliances and determines manufacturing hazards and their safeguards. Fire research began earlier in the United States and is more advanced than in Great Britain. Later they established a laboratory specializing in electrical, mechanical, hydraulic, and chemical fields.

3. When the five sentences are arranged in proper order, the paragraph starts with the sentence which begins 3.____
   A. "In 1887..." B. "Probably this..." C. "It tests..."
   D. "Fire research..." E. "Later they..."

4. In the last sentence listed above, "they" refers to 4.____
   A. the insurance companies B. the United States and Great Britain
   C. the Inspection Department D. clients
   E. technicians

5. When the above paragraph is properly arranged, it ends with the words 5.____
   A. "...and protection." B. "...the United States."
   C. "...their safeguards." D. "...in Great Britain."
   E. "...chemical fields."

---

# KEY (CORRECT ANSWERS)

1. C
2. C
3. D
4. A
5. C

---

# TEST 2

DIRECTIONS: In each of the questions numbered I through V, several sentences are given. For each question, choose as your answer the group of number that represents the MOST logical order of these sentences if they were arranged in paragraph form. *PRINT THE LETTER OF THE CORRECT ANSWER IN THE SPACE AT THE RIGHT.*

1. I. It is established when one shows that the landlord has prevented the tenant's enjoyment of his interest in the property leased. 1.____
   II. Constructive eviction is the result of a breach of the covenant of quiet enjoyment implied in all leases.
   III. In some parts of the United States, it is not complete until the tenant vacates within a reasonable time.
   IV. Generally, the acts must be of such serious and permanent character as to deny the tenant the enjoyment of his possessing rights.
   V. In this event, upon abandonment of the premises, the tenant's liability for that ceases.

   The CORRECT answer is:
   A. II, I, IV, III, V
   B. V, II, III, I, IV
   C. IV, III, I, II, V
   D. I, III, V, IV, II

2. I. The powerlessness before private and public authorities that is the typical experience of the slum tenant is reminiscent of the situation of blue-collar workers all through the nineteenth century. 2.____
   II. Similarly, in recent years, this chapter of history has been reopened by anti-poverty groups which have attempted to organize slum tenants to enable them to bargain collectively with their landlords about the conditions of their tenancies.
   III. It is familiar history that many of the worker remedied their condition by joining together and presenting their demands collectively.
   IV. Like the workers, tenants are forced by the conditions of modern life into substantial dependence on these who possess great political aid and economic power.
   V. What's more, the very fact of dependence coupled with an absence of education and self-confidence makes them hesitant and unable to stand up for what they need from those in power.

   The CORRECT answer is:
   A. V, IV, I, II, III
   B. II, III, I, V, IV
   C. III, I, V, IV, II
   D. I, IV, V, III, II

3. I. A railroad, for example, when not acting as a common carrier may contract away responsibility for its own negligence. 3.____
   II. As to a landlord, however, no decision has been found relating to the legal effect of a clause shifting the statutory duty of repair to the tenant.
   III. The courts have not passed on the validity of clauses relieving the landlord of this duty and liability.
   IV. They have, however, upheld the validity of exculpatory clauses in other types of contracts.

V. Housing regulations impose a duty upon the landlord to maintain leased premises in safe condition.
VI. As another example, a bailee may limit his liability except for gross negligence, willful acts, or fraud.

The CORRECT answer is:
A. II, I, VI, IV, III, V
B. I, III, IV, V, VI, II
C. III, V, I, IV, II, VI
D. V, III, IV, I, VI, II

4. I. Since there are only samples in the building, retail or consumer sales are generally eschewed by mart occupants, and in some instances, rigid controls are maintained to limit entrance to the mart only to those persons engaged in retailing. 4.____
II. Since World War I, in many larger cities, there has developed a new type of property, called the mart building.
III. It can, therefore, be used by wholesalers and jobbers for the display of sample merchandise.
IV. This type of building is most frequently a multi-storied, finished interior property which is a cross between a retail arcade and a loft building.
V. This limitation enables the mart occupants to ship the orders from another location after the retailer or dealer makes his selection from the samples.

The CORRECT answer is:
A. II, IV, III, I, V
B. IV, III, V, I, II
C. I, III, II, IV, V
D. I, IV, II, III, V

5. I. In general, staff-line friction reduces the distinctive contribution of staff personnel. 5.____
II. The conflicts, however, introduce an uncontrolled element into the managerial system.
III. On the other hand, the natural resistance of the line to staff innovations probably usefully restrains over-eager efforts to apply untested procedures on a large scale.
IV. Under such conditions, it is difficult to know when valuable ideas are being sacrificed.
V. The relatively weak position of staff, requiring accommodation to the line, tends to restrict their ability to engage in free, experimental innovation.

The CORRECT answer is:
A. IV, II, III, I, V
B. I, V, III, II, IV
C. V, III, I, II, IV
D. II, I, IV, V, III

## KEY (CORRECT ANSWERS)

1. A
2. D
3. D
4. A
5. B

# TEST 3

DIRECTIONS: Questions 1 through 4 consist of six sentences which can be arranged in a logical sequence. For each question, select the choice which places the numbered sentences in the MOST logical sequent. *PRINT THE LETTER OF THE CORRECT ANSWER IN THE SPACE AT THE RIGHT.*

1. I. The burden of proof as to each issue is determined before trial and remains upon the same party throughout the trial. 1.____
   II. The jury is at liberty to believe one witness' testimony as against a number of contradictory witnesses.
   III. In a civil case, the party bearing the burden of proof is required to prove his contention by a fair preponderance of the evidence.
   IV. However, it must be noted that a fair preponderance of evidence does not necessarily mean a greater number of witnesses.
   V. The burden of proof is the burden which rests upon one of the parties to an action to persuade the trier of the facts, generally the jury, that a proposition he asserts is true.
   VI. If the evidence is equally balanced, or if it leaves the jury in such doubt as to be unable to decide the controversy either way, judgment must be given against the party upon whom the burden of proof rests.

   The CORRECT answer is:
   A. III, II, V, IV, I, VI
   B. I, II, VI, V, III, IV
   C. III, IV, V, I, II, VI
   D. V, I, III, VI, IV, II

2. I. If a parent is without assets and is unemployed, he cannot be convicted of the crime of non-support of a child. 2.____
   II. The term "sufficient ability" has been held to mean sufficient financial ability.
   III. It does not matter if his unemployment is by choice or unavoidable circumstances.
   IV. If he fails to take any steps at all, he may be liable to prosecution for endangering the welfare of a child.
   V. Under the penal law, a parent is responsible for the support of his minor child only if the parent is "of sufficient ability."
   VI. An indigent parent may meet his obligation by borrowing money or by seeking aid under the provisions of the Social Welfare Law.

   The CORRECT answer is:
   A. VI, I, V, III, II, IV
   B. I, III, V, II, IV, VI
   C. V, II, I, III, VI, IV
   D. I, VI, IV, V, II, III

3. I. Consider, for example, the case of a rabble rouser who urges a group of twenty people to go out and break the windows of a nearby factory. 3.____
   II. Therefore, the law fills the indicated gap with the crime of inciting to riot.
   III. A person is considered guilty of inciting to riot when he urges ten or more persons to engage in tumultuous and violent conduct of a kind likely to create public alarm.
   IV. However, if he has not obtained the cooperation of at least four people, he cannot be charged with unlawful assembly.

V. The charge of inciting to riot was added to the law to cover types of conduct which cannot be classified as either the crime of "riot" or the crime of "unlawful assembly."
VI. If he acquires the acquiescence of at least four of them, he is guilty of unlawful assembly even if the project does not materialize.

The CORRECT answer is:
A. III, V, I, VI, IV, II
B. V, I, IV, VI, II, III
C. III, IV, I, V, II, VI
D. V, I, IV, VI, III, II

4. I. If, however, the rebuttal evidence presents an issue of credibility, it is for the jury to determine whether the presumption has, in fact, been destroyed. 4.____
II. Once sufficient evidence to the contrary is introduced, the presumption disappears from the trial.
III. The effect of a presumption is to place the burden upon the adversary to come forward with evidence to rebut the presumption.
IV. When a presumption is overcome and ceases to exist in the case, the fact or facts which gave rise to the presumption still remain.
V. Whether a presumption has been overcome is ordinarily a question for the court.
VI. Such information may furnish a basis for a logical inference.

The CORRECT answer is:
A. IV, VI, II, V, I, III
B. III, II, V, I, IV, VI
C. V, III, VI, IV, II, I
D. V, IV, I, II, VI, III

# KEY (CORRECT ANSWERS)

1. D
2. C
3. A
4. B

# PREPARING WRITTEN MATERIAL

# EXAMINATION SECTION

# TEST 1

DIRECTIONS: Each question consists of a sentence which may or may not be an example of good English usage. Examine each sentence, considering grammar, punctuation, spelling, capitalization, and awkwardness. Then choose the correct statement about it from the four choices below it. If the English usage in the sentence given is better than any of the changes suggested in choices B, C, or D, pick choice A. (Do not pick a choice that will change the meaning of the sentence.) *PRINT THE LETTER OF THE CORRECT ANSWER IN THE SPACE AT THE RIGHT.*

1. We attended a staff conference on Wednesday the new safety and fire rules were discussed. 1.____
   A. This is an example of acceptable writing.
   B. The words "safety," "fire," and "rules" should begin with capital letters.
   C. There should be a comma after the word "Wednesday."
   D. There should be a period after the word "Wednesday" and the word "the" should begin with a capital letter.

2. Neither the dictionary or the telephone directory could be found in the office library. 2.____
   A. This is an example of acceptable writing.
   B. The word "or" should be changed to "nor."
   C. The word "library" should be spelled "libery."
   D. The word "neither" should be changed to "either."

3. The report would have been typed correctly if the typist could read the draft. 3.____
   A. This is an example of acceptable writing.
   B. The word "would" should be removed.
   C. The word "have" should be inserted after the word "could."
   D. The word "correctly" should be changed to "correct."

4. The supervisor brought the reports and forms to an employees desk. 4.____
   A. This is an example of acceptable writing.
   B. The word "brought" should be changed to "took."
   C. There should be a comma after the word "reports" and a comma after the word "forms."
   D. The word "employees" should be spelled "employee's."

5. It's important for all the office personnel to submit their vacation schedules on time. 5.____
   A. This is an example of acceptable writing.
   B. The word "It's" should be spelled "Its."
   C. The word "their" should be spelled "they're."
   D. The word "personnel" should be spelled "personal."

6. The report, along with the accompanying documents, were submitted for review. 6.____
   A. This is an example of acceptable writing.
   B. The words "were submitted" should be changed to "was submitted."
   C. The word "accompanying" should be spelled "accompaning."
   D. The comma after the word "report" should be taken out.

7. If others must use your files, be certain that they understand how the system works, but insist that you do all the filing and refiling. 7.____
   A. This is an example of acceptable writing.
   B. There should be a period after the word "works," and the word "but" should start a new sentence.
   C. The words "filing" and "refiling" should be spelled "fileing" and "refileing."
   D. There should be a comma after the word "but."

8. The appeal was not considered because of its late arrival. 8.____
   A. This is an example of acceptable writing.
   B. The word "its" should be changed to "it's."
   C. The word "its" should be changed to "the."
   D. The words "late arrival" should be changed to "arrival late."

9. The letter must be read carefuly to determine under which subject it should be filed. 9.____
   A. This is an example of acceptable writing.
   B. The word "under" should be changed to "at."
   C. The word "determine" should be spelled "determin."
   D. The word "carefuly" should be spelled "carefully."

10. He showed potential as an office manager, but he lacked skill in delegating work. 10.____
   A. This is an example of acceptable writing.
   B. The word "delegating" should be spelled "delagating."
   C. The word "potential" should be spelled "potencial."
   D. The words "he lacked" should be changed to "was lacking."

# KEY (CORRECT ANSWERS)

| | | | |
|---|---|---|---|
| 1. | D | 6. | B |
| 2. | B | 7. | A |
| 3. | C | 8. | A |
| 4. | D | 9. | D |
| 5. | A | 10. | A |

# TEST 2

DIRECTIONS: Each question consists of a sentence which may or may not be an example of good English usage. Examine each sentence, considering grammar, punctuation, spelling, capitalization, and awkwardness. Then choose the correct statement about it from the four choices below it. If the English usage in the sentence given is better than any of the changes suggested in choices B, C, or D, pick choice A. (Do not pick a choice that will change the meaning of the sentence.) *PRINT THE LETTER OF THE CORRECT ANSWER IN THE SPACE AT THE RIGHT.*

1. The supervisor wants that all staff members report to the office at 9:00 A.M. 1.____
   A. This is an example of acceptable writing.
   B. The word "that" should be removed and the word "to" should be inserted after the word "members."
   C. There should be a comma after the word "wants" and a comma after the word "office."
   D. The word "wants" should be changed to "want" and the word "shall" should be inserted after the word "members."

2. Every morning the clerk opens the office mail and distributes it. 2.____
   A. This is an example of acceptable writing.
   B. The word "opens" should be changed to "open."
   C. The word "mail" should be changed to "letters."
   D. The word "it" should be changed to "them."

3. The secretary typed more fast on a desktop computer than on a laptop computer. 3.____
   A. This is an example of acceptable writing.
   B. The words "more fast" should be changed to "faster."
   C. There should be a comma after the words "desktop computer."
   D. The word "than" should be changed to "then."

4. The new stenographer needed a desk a computer, a chair and a blotter. 4.____
   A. This is an example of acceptable writing.
   B. The word "blotter" should be spelled "blodder."
   C. The word "stenographer" should begin with a capital letter.
   D. There should be a comma after the word "desk."

5. The recruiting officer said, "There are many different goverment jobs available." 5.____
   A. This is an example of acceptable writing.
   B. The word "There" should not be capitalized.
   C. The word "government" should be spelled "government."
   D. The comma after the word "said" should be removed.

6. He can recommend a mechanic whose work is reliable. 6.____
   A. This is an example of acceptable writing.
   B. The word "reliable" should be spelled "relyable."
   C. The word "whose" should be spelled "who's."
   D. The word "mechanic should be spelled "mecanic."

7. She typed quickly; like someone who had not a moment to lose. 7.____
   A. This is an example of acceptable writing.
   B. The word "not" should be removed.
   C. The semicolon should be changed to a comma.
   D. The word "quickly" should be placed before instead of after the word "typed."

8. She insisted that she had to much work to do. 8.____
   A. This is an example of acceptable writing.
   B. The word "insisted" should be spelled "incisted."
   C. The word "to" used in front of "much" should be spelled "too."
   D. The word "do" should be changed to "be done."

9. He excepted praise from his supervisor for a job well done. 9.____
   A. This is an example of acceptable writing.
   B. The word "excepted" should be spelled "accepted."
   C. The order of the words "well done" should be changed to "done well."
   D. There should be a comma after the word "supervisor."

10. What appears to be intentional errors in grammar occur several times in the passage. 10.____
    A. This is an example of acceptable writing.
    B. The word "occur" should be spelled "occurr."
    C. The word "appears" should be changed to "appear."
    D. The phrase "several times" should be changed to "from time to time."

# KEY (CORRECT ANSWERS)

| | | | |
|---|---|---|---|
| 1. | B | 6. | A |
| 2. | A | 7. | C |
| 3. | B | 8. | C |
| 4. | D | 9. | B |
| 5. | C | 10. | C |

# TEST 3

DIRECTIONS: Each question consists of a sentence which may or may not be an example of good English usage. Examine each sentence, considering grammar, punctuation, spelling, capitalization, and awkwardness. Then choose the correct statement about it from the four choices below it. If the English usage in the sentence given is better than any of the changes suggested in choices B, C, or D, pick choice A. (Do not pick a choice that will change the meaning of the sentence.) *PRINT THE LETTER OF THE CORRECT ANSWER IN THE SPACE AT THE RIGHT.*

1. The clerk could have completed the assignment on time if he knows where these materials were located. 1.____
   A. This is an example of acceptable writing.
   B. The word "knows" should be replaced by "had known."
   C. The word "were" should be replaced by "had been."
   D. The words "where these materials were located" should be replaced by "the location of these materials."

2. All employees should be given safety training. Not just those who accidents. 2.____
   A. This is an example of acceptable writing.
   B. The period after the word "training" should be changed to a colon.
   C. The period after the word "training" should be changed to a semicolon, and the first letter of the word "Not" should be changed to a small "n."
   D. The period after the word "training" should be changed to a comma, and the first letter of the word "Not" should be changed to a small "n."

3. This proposal is designed to promote employee awareness of the suggestion program, to encourage employee participation in the program, and to increase the number of suggestions submitted. 3.____
   A. This is an example of acceptable writing.
   B. The word "proposal" should be spelled "proposal."
   C. The words "to increase the number of suggestions submitted" should be changed to "an increase in the number of suggestions is expected."
   D. The word "promote" should be changed to "enhance" and the word "increase" should be changed to "add to."

4. The introduction of inovative managerial techniques should be preceded by careful analysis of the specific circumstances and conditions in each department. 4.____
   A. This is an example of acceptable writing.
   B. The word "technique" should be spelled "techneques."
   C. The word "inovative" should be spelled "innovative."
   D. A comma should be placed after the word "circumstances" and after the word "conditions."

5. This occurrence indicates that such criticism embarrasses him. 5.____
   A. This is an example of acceptable writing.
   B. The word “occurrence” should be spelled “occurence.”
   C. The word “criticism” should be spelled “critisism.
   D. The word “embarrasses” should be spelled “embarasses.

## KEY (CORRECT ANSWERS)

1. B
2. D
3. A
4. C
5. A

# BASIC FUNDAMENTALS OF WRITTEN COMMUNICATION

CONTENTS Page

# BASIC FUNDAMENTALS OF WRITTEN COMMUNICATION

INSTRUCTIONAL OBJECTIVES

1. Ability to write legibly.
2. Ability to fill out forms and applications correctly.
3. Ability to take messages and notes accurately.
4. Ability to write letters effectively.
5. Ability to write directions and instructions clearly.
6. Ability to outline written and spoken information.
7. Ability to persuade or teach others through written communication.
8. Ability to write effective overviews and summaries.
9. Ability to make smooth transitions within written communications.
10. Ability to use language forms appropriate for the reader.
11. Ability to prepare effective informational reports.

CONTENT

INTRODUCTION

Public-service employees are required to prepare written communications for a variety of purposes. Written communication is a fundamental tool, not only for the public-service occupations, but throughout the world of work. Many public-service occupations require written communication with ordinary citizens of diverse backgrounds, so the trainee should develop the ability to write in simple, nontechnical language that the ordinary citizen will understand.

This unit is designed to develop the student's ability to communicate effectively in writing for a number of different purposes and in a number of different formats. Whatever the particular purpose or format, how·· ever, effective writing will require the writer:

- to have a clear idea of his purpose and his audience;
- to organize his thoughts and information in an orderly way;
- to express himself concisely, accurately, and concretely;
- to report relevant facts;
- to explain and summarize ideas clearly; and
- to evaluate the effectiveness of his communication.

1. BUSINESS WRITING

Several forms of written communication tend to recur frequently in most public-service agencies, including:

- letters
- forms
- memoranda
- minutes of meetings
- short reports
- telegrams and cables
- news releases
- and many others

The public-service employee should be familiar with the principles of writing in these forms, and should be able to apply them in preparing effective communications.

Letters

Every letter sent from a public-service agency should be considered an ambassador of goodwill. The impression it creates may mean the difference between favorable public attitudes or unfavorable ones. It may mean the difference between creating a friend or an enemy for the agency. Every public-service employee has a responsibility to serve the public effectively and to provide services in an efficient and courteous manner. The letters an agency sends out reflect its attitudes toward the public.

The impression a letter creates depends upon both its appearance and its tone. A letter which shows erasures and pen written corrections gives an impression that the sending agency is slovenly. Similarly, a rude or impersonal letter creates the impression that the agency is insensitive or unfeeling. In preparing letters, the employee should apply principles of style and tone which will serve to create the most favorable impression.

*Select the Letter Type*. The two most common types of business letters are letters of inquiry and letters of response - that is, "asking" letters and "answering" letters. Whichever type of letter the employee is asked to write, the following guidelines will simplify the task and help to achieve a style and tone which will create a favorable impression on the reader.

*Select the Right Format*. Several styles of letter format are in common use today, including:

- the indented format,
- the block format, and
- the semi-block format.

Modified forms of these are also in use in some offices. The student should become familiar with the formats preferred for usage in his office, and be able to use whichever form the employer requests.

*Know the Letter Elements*. Every letter includes certain basic elements, such as:

- the letterhead, which identifies the name and address of the sender.
- the date on which the letter was transmitted.
- the inside address, with the name, street, city, and state of the addressee.
- the salutation, greeting the addressee.
- the body, containing the message.
- the complimentary close, the "good-bye" of the business letter.
- the signature, handwritten by the sender.
- the typed signature, the typewritten name and title of the sender.

In addition, several other elements are occasionally found in business letters:

- the *attention line,* directing the letter to the attention of a particular individual or his representative.
- the *subject line,* informing the reader at a glance of the subject of the letter.

- the *enclosure notation,* noting items enclosed with the letter.
- the *copy notation,* listing other persons who receive copies of the letter.
- the *postscript,* an afterthought sometimes (but not normally) added following the last typed line of the letter.

Be *Brief.* Use only the words which help to say what is needed in a clear and straightforward manner. Do not repeat information already known to the reader, or contained elsewhere in the letter. Likewise, do not repeat information contained in the letter being answered. Rather than repeat the content of a previous letter, one can say something like, "Please refer to our letter dated March 5:"

An employee can shorten his letters by using single words that serve the same function as longer phrases. Many commonly used phrases can be replaced by single words. For example,

| Phrase | Single word |
|---|---|
| in order to | to |
| in reference to in | about |
| the amount of | for, of |
| in a number of cases | some |
| in view of | because |
| with regard to | about, in |

Similarly, avoid the use of adjectives and nouns that are formed from verbs. If the root verbs are used instead, the writing will be more concise and more vivid. For example,

| Noun form | Verb form |
|---|---|
| We made an adjustment on our books | We adjusted our books |
| We are sorry we cannot make a replacement of | We are sorry we cannot replace |
| Please make a correction in our order | Please correct our order |

Be on the lookout for unnecessary adjectives and adverbs which tend to clutter letters without adding information or improving style. Such unnecessary words tend to distract the reader and make it more difficult for him to grasp the main points. Observe how the superfluous words, italicized in the following example, obscure the meaning: "You may be *very much* disappointed to learn that the *excessively large* demand for our *highly popular recent* publication, 'Your Income Taxes,' has led to an *unexpected* shortage of this *attractive* publication and we *sadly* expect they will not be replenished until *quite* late this year."

Summarizing, then, a *good letter is simple and clear, with short, simple words, sentences, and paragraphs. Related parts* of *sentences and paragraphs are kept together and placed in an order which makes it easy for the reader to follow the main thoughts.*

*Be Natural*. Whenever possible, use a human touch. Use names and personal pronouns to let the reader know the letter was written by a person, not an institution. Instead of saying, "It is the policy of this agency to contact its clients once each year to confirm their status," try this: "Our policy, Mr. Jones, is to confirm your status once each year."

*Use Concrete Nouns*. Avoid using abstract words and generalizations. Use names of objects, places, and persons rather than abstractions.

*Use Active verbs*. The passive voice gives a motionless, weak tone to most writing. Instead of "The minutes were taken by Mrs. Smith," say, "Mrs. Smith took the minutes." Instead of "The plans were prepared by the banquet committee," say, "The banquet committee prepared the plans."

*Use a Natural Tone*. Many people tend to become hard, cold, and unnatural the moment they write a letter. *Communicating by letter should have the same natural tone of conversation used in everyday speech.* One way to achieve a natural and personal tone in the majority of letters is through the use of personal pronouns. Instead of saying, "Referring to your letter of March 5, reporting the non-receipt of goods ordered last February 15, please be advised that the goods were shipped as requested," say, "I am sorry to hear that you failed to receive the items you ordered last February 15. We shipped them the same day we received your letter."

## Forms

In most businesses and public service agencies, repetitive work is simplified by the use of *forms*. Forms exist for nearly every purpose imaginable: for ordering supplies, preparing invoices, applying for jobs, applying for insurance, paying taxes, recording inventories, and so on. While the forms encountered in different agencies may differ widely, several principles should be applied in completing any form:

- *Legibility*. Entries on forms should be clear and legible. Print or type wherever possible. When space provided is insufficient, attach a supplementary sheet to the form.

- *Completeness*. Make an entry in every space provided on the form. If a particular space does not apply to the applicant, enter there the term "N/A" (for "not applicable"). The reader of the completed form will then know that the applicant did not simply overlook that space.

- *Conciseness*. Forms are intended to elicit a maximum amount of information in the least possible space. When completing a form, it is usually not necessary to write complete sentences. Provide the necessary information in the least possible words.

- Accuracy. Be sure the information provided on the form is accurate. If the entry is a number, such as a social security number or an address, double-check the correctness of the number. Be sure of the spelling of names, No one appreciates receiving a communication in which his name is misspelled.

Memoranda

The written communications passing between offices or departments are usually transmitted in a form known as *"interoffice memorandum."* The headings most often used on such "memos" are:

- TO: identifying the addressee,
- FROM: identifying the sender or the originating office,
- SUBJECT: identifying briefly the subject of the memo,
- DATE: identifying the date the memo was prepared.

Larger agencies may also use headings such as FILE or REFERENCE NO. to aid in filing and retrieving memoranda.

In writing a memo, many of the same rules for letter-writing may be applied. Both the appearance and tone of the memo should create a pleasing impression. The format should be neat and follow the standards set by the originating office. The tone should be friendly, courteous, and considerate. The language should be clear, concise, and complete.

Memos usually dispense with salutations, complimentary closings, and signatures of the writers. In most other respects, however, the memorandum will follow the rules of good letter-writing.

Minutes of Meetings

Most formal public-service organization conduct meetings from time to time at which group decisions are made about agency policies, procedures, and work assignments. The records of such meetings are called *minutes.*

Minutes should be written as clearly and simply as possible, summarizing only the essential facts and decisions made at the meeting. While some issue may have been discussed at great length, only the final decision or resolution made of it should be recorded in the minutes. Information of this sort is usually included:

- Time and place of the call to order,
- Presiding officer and secretary,
- Voting members present (with names, if a small organization),

- Approval and corrections of previous minutes,
- Urgent business,
- Old business,
- New business,
- Time of adjournment,
- Signature of recorder.

Minutes should be written in a factual and objective style. The opinions of the recorder should not be in evidence. Every item of business coming up before a meeting should be included in the minutes, together with its disposition. For example:

- "M/S/P (Moved, seconded, passed) that Mr. Thomas Jones take responsibility for rewriting the personnel procedures manual."
- "Discussion of the summer vacation schedule was tabled until the next meeting."
- "M/S/P, a resolution that no client of the agency should be kept waiting more than 20 minutes for an interview."

Note that considerable discussion may have surrounded each of the above items in the minutes, but that only the topic and its resolution are recorded.

Short Reports

The public-service employee often is called upon to prepare a short report gathering and interpreting information on a single topic. Reports of this kind are sometimes prepared so that all the relevant information may be assembled in one place to aid the organization in making certain decisions. Such reports may be read primarily by the staff of the organization or by others closely related to the decision-making process.

Reports may be prepared at other times for distribution to the public or to other agencies and institutions. These reports may serve the purpose of informing public opinion or persuading others on matters of public policy.

Whatever the purpose of the short report, its physical appearance and style of presentation should be designed to create a favorable impression on the reader. Even if the report is distributed only within the writer's own unit, an attractive, clear, thorough report will reflect the writer's dedication to his assignment and the pride he takes in his work.

Some guidelines which will assist the trainee in preparation of effective short reports include use of the following:

- A good quality paper;
- Wide and even margins, allowing binding room;

- An accepted standard style of typing;
- A title page;
- A table of contents (for more lengthy reports only);
- A graphic numbering or outlining system, if needed for clarity;
- Graphics and photos to clarify meaning when useful;
- Footnotes, used sparingly, and only when they contribute to the report;
- A bibliography of sources, using a standard citation style.

A discussion of the organization of content for informational reports follows later in this document.

News Releases

From time to time, the public-service employees may be called upon to prepare a news release for his agency. Whenever the activities of the agency are newsworthy or of interest to the public, the agency has an obligation to report such activities to the press. The most common means for such reporting is by using the press release. Most newspapers and broadcasting stations are initially informed of agencies' activities by news releases distributed by the agencies themselves. Thus, the news release is a basic tool for communicating with the public served by the agency.

The news release is written in news style, with these basic characteristics:

- Sentences are short and simple.
- Paragraphs are short (one or two sentences) and relate to a single item of information.
- Paragraphs are arranged in *inverted order*—the most important in information appears first.
- The first or *lead* paragraph summarizes the entire story. If the reader went no further, he would have the essential information.
- Subsequent paragraphs provide further details, the most important occurring first.
- Reported information is attributed to sources; that is, the source of the news is reported in the story.
- The expression of the writer's opinions is scrupulously avoided.
- The 5 W's (who, what, why, where, when) are included.

News releases should be typed double spaced on standard 8 1/2 x 11 paper, with generous margins and at least 2" of open space above the lead paragraph. Do not write headlines - that is the editor's job. At the top of the first page of the release include the name of the agency releasing the story and the name and phone number of the person to contact if more information is needed. If the release runs more than one page, end each page with the word "-more-" to indicate that more copy follows. End the release with the symbols "###" to indicate that the copy ends at that point.

Accuracy and physical appearance are essential characteristics of the news release. Typographical errors, or errors of fact, such as misspelled names, lead editors to doubt the reliability of the story. Great care should be taken to assure the accuracy and reliability of a news release.

2. REPORTING ON A TOPIC

At one time or another, most public-service employees will be asked to prepare a report on some topic. Usually the need for the report grows out of some policy decision contemplated by the agency for which full information must be considered. For example:

- Should the agency undertake some new project or service?
- Should working conditions be changed?
- Are new specialists needed on the staff?
- Or should a branch office be opened up?

Or any of a hundred other such decisions which the agency must make from time to time.

When called upon to prepare such a report, the employee should have a model to follow which will guide his collection of information and will help him to prepare an effective and useful report.

As with other forms of written communication, both the physical appearance and content of the report are important to create a favorable impression and to engender confidence. The physical appearance of such reports has been discussed earlier; additional suggestions for reports are given in Unit 3. Basic guidelines follow below for organizing and preparing the content.

Preparation for the Report

*What is the Purpose of the Report?* The preparer of the report should have clearly in mind why the report is needed:

- What is the decision being contemplated by the agency?
- To what use will the report be put?

Before beginning to prepare the report, the writer should discuss its purpose fully with the decision-making staff to articulate the purpose the report is intended to serve. If the employee is himself initiating the report, it would be well to discuss its purpose with colleagues to assure that its purpose is clear in his own mind.

*What Questions Should the Report Answer?* Once the purpose of the report is clear, the questions the report must answer may begin to become clear. For example, if the decision faced by the agency is whether or not to offer a new service, questions may be asked such as these:

- What persons would be served by the new service?

- What would the new service cost?
- What new staff would be needed?
- What new equipment and facilities would be needed?
- What alternative ways exist for offering the service?
- How might the new service be administered?

And so on. Unless the purpose of the report is clear, it is difficult to decide what specific questions need to be answered. Once the purpose is clear, these questions can be specified.

*Where Can the Relevant Information be Obtained?* Once the questions are clear in the writer's mind, he can identify the information he will need to answer them. Information may usually be obtained from two general sources:

- *Relevant documents.* Records, publications, and other reports are often useful in locating the information needed to answer particular questions. These may be in the files of the writer's own agency, in other agencies, or in libraries.

- *Personal contacts.* Persons in a position to know the needed information may be contacted in person, by phone, or by letter. Such contacts are especially important in obtaining firsthand accounts of previous experience.

The Text of the Report

*What are the Answers to the Questions?* Once the relevant in-formation is in hand, the answers to the questions may be assembled.

- What does the information reveal? This activity amounts to summarizing the information obtained. It often helps to organize this summary around the specific questions asked by the report. For example, if the report asks in one part, "What are the costs of the new service likely to be?" one section of the report should summarize the information gathered to answer this question.

*Organizing the Report.* The organization of a report into main and subsections depends upon the nature of the report. Reports will differ widely in their organization and treatment. In general, however, the report should generally follow the pattern previously discussed. That is, reports which generally include the following subjects in order will be found to be clear in their intent and to communicate effectively:

- *Description of problem or purpose.* Example: "One problem facing our agency is whether or not we should extend our hours of operation to better serve the public. This report is intended to examine the problem and make recommendations."

- *Questions to be answered.* Example: "In examining this problem, answers were sought to the following questions: What persons would be served? What would it cost? What staff would be needed?"

- *Information sources.* Example: "To answer these questions, letters of complaint for the past three years were examined. Interviews with clients were conducted by phone and in person, phone interviews were conducted with the agency directors in Memphis, Philadelphia, and Chicago,"

- *Summary of findings.* Example: "At least 25 percent of the agency's clients would be served better by evening or Saturday service. The costs of operating eight hours of extended service would be negligible, since the service could be provided by rescheduling work assignments. The present staff report they would be inconvenienced by evening and Saturday work assignments."

*The Writer's Responsibilities.* It is the writer's responsibility to address finally the original purpose of the report. Once the questions have been answered, an informed judgment can be made as to the decision facing the agency. It is at this stage that the writer attempts to draw conclusions from the information he has gathered and summarized. For example, if the original purpose of the report was to help make a decision about whether or not the agency should offer a new service, the writer should draw conclusions from the information and recommend either for or against the new service.

*Conclusions and Recommendations.* Example: "It appears that operating during extended hours would better serve a significant number of clients. The writer recommends that the agency offer this new service. The present staff should be given temporary assignments to cover the extended hours. As new staff are hired to replace separating persons, they should be hired specifically to cover the extended hours."

## 3. PERSUASIVE WRITING

Often in life, people are called upon to persuade individuals and groups to adopt ideas believed to be good, or attitudes favorable to ideas thought to be worthwhile or behavior believed to be beneficial. The public service employee may find he must persuade the staff of his own agency, his superiors, the clients of the agency, or the general public in his community.

Persuading others by means of written and other forms of communication is a difficult task and requires much practice. Some principles have emerged from the study of persuasion which may provide some guidelines for developing a model for persuasive writing.

General Guidelines for Writing Persuasively

*Know the Credibility of the Source*. People are more likely to be persuaded by a message they perceive originates from a trustworthy source. Their trust is enhanced if the source is seen as authoritative, or knowledgeable on the issue discussed in the message. Their trust is increased also if the source appears to have nothing to gain either way, has no vested interest in the final decision. Then, the assertions made in persuasive writing should be backed up by referencing trustworthy and disinterested information sources.

*Avoid Overemotional Appeals*. Appealing to the common emotions of man—love, hate, tear, sex, etc.—can have a favorable effect on the outcome of a persuasive message. But care should be taken because, if the appeal is too strong, it can lead to a reverse effect. For example, if an agency wanted to persuade the public to get chest X-rays, it would have much greater chance of success if it adopted a positive and helpful attitude rather than trying to frighten them into this action. For instance, appealing mildly to the sense of well-being which accompanies knowledge of one's own good health, instead of shocking the public by showing horror pictures of patients who died from lack of timely X-rays.

*Consider the Other Man's Point of View*. To persuade another to one's own point of view, should the writer include information and arguments contrary to his own position? Or should he argue only for his own side?

Generally, it depends on where most of the audience stand in the first place. If most of the audience already favor the position being advocated, then the writer will probably do better including only information favorable to his position. However, if the greater part of the audience are likely to oppose this position, then the writer would probably be better off including their arguments also. In this case, he may be helping his cause by rebutting the opposing arguments as he introduces them into the writing.

An example of this technique might occur in arguing for such an idea as a four-day, forty-hour workweek. Thus: "Many people feel that the ten-hour day is too long and that they would arrive home too late for their regular dinner hour. But think! If you have dinner a littler later each night, you'll have a three-day weekend every week. More days free to go fishing, or camping. More days with your wife and children." That is good persuasive writing!

Interpersonal Communications

The important role of interpersonal communication in persuading others—face-to-face and person-to-person communications—has been well documented. Mass mailings or printed messages will likely have less effect than personal letters and conversations between persons already known to each other. In any persuasion campaign the personal touch is very important.

An individual in persuading a large number of persons will likely be more effective if he can organize a letter-writing campaign of persuasive messages written by persons favorable to his position to their friends and acquaintances, than if his campaign is based upon sending out a mass mailing of a printed message.

Conditions for Persuading. In order for an audience of one or many to be persuaded in the manner desired, these conditions must be met:

- the audience must be *exposed* to the message,
- members of the audience must *perceive* the intent of the message,
- they must *remember* the message afterwards,
- each member must *decide* whether or not to adopt the ideas.

Each member of the audience will respond to a message differently. While every person may receive the message, not everyone will read it. Even among those who read it, not everyone will perceive it in the same way. Some will remember it longer than others. Not everyone will decide to adopt the ideas. These effects are called *selective exposure, selective perception, selective retention,* and *selective decision.*

The Persuasion Campaign. How can one counteract these selective effects in persuading others? One thing that is known is that *people tend to be influenced by persuasive messages which they are already predisposed to accept.* This means a person is more likely to persuade people a little than to persuade them a lot.

In planning a persuasion campaign, therefore, the messages should be tailored to the audiences. Success will be more likely if one starts with people who believe *almost* as the writer wants to persuade them to believe—people who are most likely to agree with the position advocated.

The writer also wants to use arguments based on values the particular audience already accepts. For example, in advocating a new teenage job program, he might argue with business men that the program will help business; with parents, that it will build character; with teachers, that it is educational; with taxpayers, that it will reduce future taxes; and so on.

*The idea is to find some way to make sure that each member of the particular audiences reached can see an advantage for himself, and for the writer to then tailor the messages for those audiences.*

4. INSTRUCTIONAL WRITING

Another task that the public-service employee may expect to face from time to time is the instruction of some other person in the performance of a task. This may sometimes involve preparing written instructions to other employees in the unit, or preparing a training manual for new employees.

It may sometimes involve preparing instructional manuals for clients of the unit, such as "How to Apply for a Real Estate License," "How to Bathe your Baby," or "How to Recognize the Symptoms of Heart Disease."

Whatever the purpose or the audience, certain principles of instruction may be applied which will help make more effective these instructional or training communications. These are: *advance organizers, practice, errorless learning,* and *feedback.*

Advance Organizers

At or near the beginning of an instructional communication, it helps the learner if he is provided with what can be called an "advance organizer." This element of the communication performs two functions:

- it provides a framework or "map" for the leader to organize the information he will encounter,
- it helps the learner perceive his purpose in learning the tasks which will follow.

The first paragraphs in this section, for example, serve together as an advance organizer. The trainee is informed that he may be called upon to perform these tasks in his job *(perceived purpose),* and that he will be instructed in advance organizers, practice, errorless learning, and feedback *(framework, or "map").*

Practice

The notion of *practice makes perfect* is a sound instructional principle. When trying to teach someone to perform a task by means of written communication, the writer should build in many opportunities for practicing the task, or parts of it. This built-in practice should be both appropriate and active:

- *Appropriate practice* is practice which is directly related to learning the tasks at hand.

- *Active practice* is practice in actually performing the task at hand or parts of it, rather than simply reading about the task, or thinking about it.

By inserting questions into the text of the communication, by giving practice quizzes, exercises, or field work, one can build into his instructional communication the kind of practice necessary for the reader to readily learn the task.

Errorless Learning

The practice given learners should be easy to do. That is, they should not be asked to practice a task if they are likely to make a lot of mistakes. When a mistake is practiced it is likely to recur again and again, like spelling "demons," which have been spelled wrong so often it's difficult to recall the way they should be spelled. Because it is better to practice a task right from the first, it is important that learners do not make errors in practice.

- One method for encouraging correct practice is to give the reader hints, or *prompts,* to help him practice correctly.
- Another method is to instruct him in a logical sequence a little bit at a time. Don't try to teach everything at once. Break the task down into small parts and teach each part of the task in order. Then give the learner practice in each part of the task before giving him practice in the whole thing.
- A third way of encouraging errorless learning is to build in practice and review throughout the communication. The learner may forget part of the task if the teacher doesn't review it with him from time to time.

Remember, people primarily learn from what they do, so build in to the instructional communication many opportunities for the learner to practice correctly all of the parts of the task required for learning, first separately and then all together.

Feedback

The reader, or learner, can't judge how well he is learning the task unless he is informed of it. In a classroom situation, the teacher usually confirms that the learner has been successful, or points out the errors he made, and provides additional instruction. An instructional communication can also help learners in the same way, by providing *feedback* to the learner.

Following practice, the writer should include in his instructional communication information which will let the reader know whether he performed the task correctly. In case he didn't, the writer should also include some further information which will help the reader perform it correctly next time. This feedback, then, performs two functions:

- it helps the learner confirm that his practice was done correctly, and
- it helps him correct his performance of the task in case he made any errors.

Feedback will be most helpful to the learner if it occurs immediately following practice. The learner should be brought to know of his success or his errors just as soon as possible after practice.

STUDENT LEARNING ACTIVITIES

- Write "asking" and "answering" letters, and answer a letter of complaint, using the format assigned by the teacher.
- Write memoranda to other "offices" in a fictitious organization. Plan a field trip using only memos to communicate with other students in the class.
- Take minutes of a small group meeting. Or attend a meeting of the school board and take minutes.
- Write a short report on a public service occupation of special interest to you.
- Write a 15-word telegram reserving a single room at a hotel and asking to be picked up at the airport.
- Write a news release announcing a new service offered to the public by your agency.
- Based upon hearing a reading or pretaping of a report, summarize the report in news style.
- View films on effective communication, for example, *Getting the Facts, Words that Don't Inform,* and *A Message to No One.*
- For a given problem or purpose, compile a list of specific questions you would need to answer to write a report on the topic.
- For a given list of questions, discuss and compile a list of information sources relevant to the questions.
- As a member of a group, consider the problem of "What field trip should the class take to help students learn how to write an effective news release?" What questions will you need to answer? Where will you obtain your information?
- As a member of a group, gather the information and prepare a short report based on it for presentation to the class.
- Write a report on a problem assigned by your teacher.
- Write a brief persuasive letter to a friend on a given topic. Assume he does not already agree with you. Apply principles of source credibility, emotional appeals, and one or both sides of the issue to persuade him.

- Plan a persuasive campaign to persuade a given segment of your community to take some given action.
- Write a short instructional communication on a verbal learning task assigned by your teacher.
- Write a short instructional communication on a learning task which involves the operation of equipment.
- Try your instructional communications with a fellow student to check for errors during practice.

TEACHER MANAGEMENT ACTIVITIES

- Have students practice letter writing. Assign letters of "asking" and "answering." Read them a letter of complaint and ask them to write an answering letter. Establish common rules of format and style for each assignment. Change the rules from time to time to give practice in several styles.
- Have small groups plan an event, such as a field trip, assigning the various tasks to one another using only memoranda. Evaluate the effectiveness of each group's memo writing by the speed and completeness of their planning.
- Have the class attend a public meeting. Assign each the task of taking the minutes. Evaluate the minutes for brevity and completeness.
- Encourage each student to prepare a short report on a public service occupation of special interest to himself.
- Give the students practice in writing 15-word telegrams.
- Have the students prepare a news release announcing some new service offered to the public, such as "Taxpayers can now obtain help from the Internal Revenue Service in completing their income tax forms as a result of a new service now being offered by the agency."
- Give the students practice in summarizing and writing leads by giving them the facts of a news event and asking them to write a one or two-sentence lead summarizing the significant facts of the event.
- Read a speech or a story. Have students write a summary and a report of the speech or story in news style.
- Show films on effective communication, for example, *Getting the Facts, Words that Don't Inform,* and *A Message to No One.*
- State a general problem and have each student prepare a list of the specific questions implied by the problem.

- State a list of specific questions and discuss with the class the sources of information which might bear upon each of the questions.

- Have small groups consider and write short reports jointly on the general problem, "What field trip should the class take to help students learn how to write an effective news release?" Have each group identify the specific questions to be answered, with sources for needed information.

- Have each student identify and prepare a short report on a general problem of interest.

- Assign students to work in groups of three or four to draft a letter to a friend to persuade him to make a contribution to establish a new city art museum.

- Assign the students to groups of five or six, each group to map out a persuasive campaign on a given topic. Some topics are "Give Blood," "Get Chest X-Ray," "Quit Smoking," "Don't Litter," "Inspect Your House Wiring," etc.

- Have each student identify a simple verbal learning task and prepare an instructional communication to teach that task to another student not familiar with the task.

- Have each student prepare an instructional manual designed to train someone to operate some simple piece of equipment, such as an adding machine, a slide projector, a tape recorder, or something of similar complexity.

- Have each student try his instructional communication out on another student, unfamiliar with the task. He should observe the activities and responses of the trial student to identify errors made in practice. He should revise the communication, adding practice, review, and prompts wherever needed to reduce errors in practice.

# EVALUATION QUESTIONS

## Written Communications

1. Which type of letter would be correct for a public service worker to send? 1.____

    A. A letter containing erasures
    B. A letter reflecting goodwill
    C. A rude letter
    D. An impersonal letter

2. Memos usually leave out: 2.____

    A. Complimentary closings
    B. The name of the sender
    C. The name of the addressee
    D. The date the memo was sent

3. A good business letter would not contain: 3.____

    A. Short, simple words, sentences, and paragraphs
    B. Information contained in the letter being answered
    C. Concrete nouns and active verbs
    D. Orderly placed paragraphs

4. In writing business letters it is important to: 4.____

    A. Use a conversational tone
    B. Use a hard, cold tone
    C. Use abstract words
    D. Use a passive tone

5. Messages between departments in an agency are usually sent by: 5.____

    A. Letter
    B. Memo
    C. Telegram
    D. Long reports

6. Repetitive work can be simplified by the use of: 6.____

    A. Memos
    B. Telegrams
    C. Forms
    D. Reports

7. In filling out forms and applications, it is important to be: 7.____

    A. Legible
    B. Complete
    C. Accurate
    D. All of the above

8. Memos should be: 8.___

A. Clear
B. Brief
C. Complete
D. All of the above

9. Minutes of meetings should not include: 9.___

A. The opinions of the recorder
B. The approval of previous minutes
C. The corrections of previous minutes
D. The voting members present

10. Reports are written by public service workers to: 10.___

A. Assemble information in one place
B. Aid the organization in making decisions
C. Inform the public and other agencies
D. All of the above

11. News releases should include: 11.___

A. A lead paragraph summarizing the story
B. Long paragraphs about many topics
C. The writer's opinion
D. All of the above

12. Readers of news releases and reports are influenced by the: 12.___

A. Content of the material
B. Accuracy of the material
C. Physical appearance of the material
D. All of the above

13. The contents of a report should include: 13.___

A. A description of the problem
B. The questions to be answered
C. Unimportant information
D. A summary of findings

14. People tend to be influenced easier if: 14.___

A. They can see something in the position that would be advantageous to them
B. They are almost ready to agree anyhow
C. The appeal to the emotions is not overly strong
D. All of the above

# KEY (CORRECT ANSWERS)

1. B
2. A
3. B
4. A
5. B
6. C
7. D
8. D
9. A
10. D
11. A
12. D
13. C
14. D

# GLOSSARY OF TERMS UNDER THE WORKERS' COMPENSATION DISABILITY BENEFITS VOLUNTEER FIREFIGHTERS' BENEFIT LAWS

## CONTENTS

# GLOSSARY OF TERMS
# UNDER THE WORKERS' COMPENSATION DISABILITY BENEFITS VOLUNTEER FIREFIGHTERS' BENEFIT LAWS

## A

ACCIDENT, NOTICE AND CAUSAL RELATIONSHIP - (W). The finding made by presiding Referee or the Board that the claimant "sustained an accidental injury arising out of and in the course of employment; that he gave timely notice thereof to his employer; and that the disability is causally related to the accidental injury. (Sec. 2, Subd., 7; Sec. 18)

ACCIDENTAL INJURY - (W). A personal injury which is accidental and which arose out of and in the course of employment, and such disease or infection as may naturally and unavoidably result there from. The term implies an unlocked for mishap or untoward event, and should be construed in line with the common sense view of the average man. (Sec. 2, Subd. 7)

ACTUAL REDUCED EARNINGS (ARE) - (W). The difference between the claimant's post-accident earnings and his pre-accident earnings. (Sec. 14)

ADJOURNMENT ASSESSMENT - (A). A $25.00 assessment which the Board may impose in its discretion for each adjourned hearing held at the request of the carrier.

AFFIDAVIT - (A). A written statement under oath or affirmation made or taken before an officer having authority to administer such oath.

AGGREGATE TRUST FUND - (W). An indivisible trust fund established under Section 27 to assure the payment of worker's compensation in claims involving permanent total disability, the loss of major memb case and fatal injuries. A private carrier is required and a self-insured employer under certain circumstances is permitted to pay the actuarial value of a claimant's future compensation payments in the above type case into the fund, and upon such payment, the carrier and the self-insured employer are discharged from further liability to such claimant for compensation or death benefits. (Section 27).

ANCR - (W). The abbreviation for ACCIDENT, NOTICE AND CAUSAL RELATIONSHIP. See explanation of the Findings under "Accident, Notice and Causal Relationship," above.

APPEAL - (A). The legal action taken by one of the parties in the Appellate Division, Third Department, to reverse or amend a decision or direction made by a Board Panel or the imposition of an assessment made by the Chairman, Worker's Compensation Board, pursuant to Section 52 (5) of the Law. (Sections 23, 224, W.C.L. and Section 46, V.F.B.L.)

APPLICATION FOR REVIEW - (A). A written request to the Worker's Compensation Board for modification or rescission or review of an award or decision of a Referee, specifying the grounds on which it is made. It must be filed within 30 days after notice of the filing of the decision sought to be reviewed, and should be directed to the Worker's Compensation Board. (Sections 23,224, Board Rule 13 W.C.L. and Section 46, V.F.B.L.)

ARISING OUT OF AN IN THE COURSE OF EMPLOYMENT - (W). The injury that "arises out of" the employment is one that was caused by a hazard of the employment. The injury that is "in the course of employment" is one that arose at a time, place and under circumstances related to the employment. Both conditions must be satisfied in order to establish a work-connected accidental injury. (Section 2, Subd. 7)

AUTHORIZED PHYSICIAN - (A). A physician licensed to practice medicine in the State of New York who has been authorized by the Chairman of the Workers' Compensation Board to render medical care or treatment under the Workers' Compensation Law. The authorization specifies the character of the medical care which the physician is authorized to render. (Section 13-b, Subd. 2; Reg. 110)

AUTHORIZED PODIATRIST - (A). A podiatrist licensed to practice podiatry in the State of New York who has been authorized by the Chairman of the Workers' Compensation Board to render podiatric care or-treatment under the Workers' Compensation Law. When care is required for injury to the foot, the injured worker may select to treat him any authorized physician or podiatrist. (Section 13-k; Reg. 110)

AUTHORIZED CHIROPRACTOR - (A). A chiropractor licensed to practice chiropractic in the State of New York who has been authorized by the Chairman of the Workers' Compensation Board to render chiropractic care under the Workers' Compensation Law within the limits prescribed by the Education Law.

AVERAGE WEEKLY WAGE - (W). The average weekly wage is one-fifty second part of the average annual earnings of the injured worker. Such average annual earnings are computed in one of the following ways: If the claimant worked in the employment in which he was injured, substantially the whole year preceding the injury, whether for the same employer or not, his average annual earnings will consist of three hundred times his average daily wage if he was a six-day worker, and two-hundred and sixty times his average daily wage if he was a five-day worker. A claimant who has worked ninety percent of the year preceding the injury, is deemed to have worked substantially the whole of the year. In the event the claimant has not worked a substantial part of the year, the average daily wage of another employee of the same class, who has worked substantially the whole of such immediately preceding year in the same or similar employment, in the same or a neighboring area will be used to fix the claimant's average annual earnings. Where the employment itself as distinguished from the claimant's relationship to it, is intermittent or discontinuous, and the multiplication of claimant's average daily wage by either the three-hundred multiple or the two-hundred and sixty multiple will not accurately reflect his annual earning capacity, the claimant's average annual earnings will be fixed at two-hundred times his average daily wage in the employment in which he was injured. (Section 14)

AVERAGE WEEKLY WAGE - (D). The amount determined by dividing the total wages of an employee in the employment of his last covered employer for the eight weeks or portion thereof that the employee was in such employment immediately preceding and including his last day worked prior to the commencement of such disability, by the number of weeks or portion thereof of such employment. (Section 201, Subd. 12)

## B

BINDER - (A). A temporary insurance contract which, except for specified differences, contains the terms of the contract which will replace it. The binder obligates the carrier to fulfill the terms of the contract just as if the final contract were in effect.

BOARD OF CONSULTANTS - (W). Two compensation examining physicians appointed by the Board Medical Director to examine a claimant when objection is taken to the report of another compensation examining physician in schedule type cases exclusive of eye and ear cases.

BOARD DENIAL - (A). A Board decision denying the relief sought in an application for review of a Referee decision because the record developed at the Referee hearing(s) supports the Referee decision. (Sections 23, 224)

BOARD PANEL - (A). A panel of three Board Members who render decisions on applications for review of Referee decisions. The decision of a Board Panel is deemed the decision of the Board. (Section 142)

BOARD REVIEW - (A). Where a Referee decision is disputed, the aggrieved party may file an application for a review thereof with the Board. The Board's decision on the application will contain a statement of the facts which formed the basis of its action on the issue raised. Appeals from Board decisions may be taken to the Appellate Division of the Supreme Court, Third Department, and thereafter to the Court of Appeals. (Sections 23, 224, Board Rule 13)

## C

CALENDAR - (A). A list of cases scheduled to be heard on a given date at a specific part or hearing point. (Section 141; Board Rules 4, 7, 8, and 9)

CARRIER - (W.V). The term applies to the State Fund, stock corporations, mutual corporations or reciprocal insurers with which employers cover their liability under the Workers' Compensation Law, the Disability Benefits Law and the Volunteer Firefighters' Benefit Law. The term also applies to self-insured employers. The carrier is liable for the payment of benefits and where indicated, medical care. (Section 2, Subd. 12; Section 50, Subd. 3)

CARRIER - (D). The term applies to the State Fund, stock or mutual corporations, and reciprocal insurers which insure the payment of disability benefits; and employers and associations of employers or of employees and trustees authorized or permitted to pay benefits. (Section 201, Subd. 11)

CAUSAL RELATIONSHIP - (W,V). The connection between the claimant's physical condition and his accidental injury or occupational disease. (Section 2, Subd. 7)

CHIROPRACTIC FEE SCHEDULE - (W.V.). The schedule established by the Chairman of the Workers' Compensation Board of changes and fees for chiropractic treatment and care furnished to workers' compensation claimants. (Section 13-1).

CLAIM - (W). A request on a prescribed form C-3 for workers' compensation for work-connected injury, occupational disease disablement, or death (form C-62) resulting from either cause. A claimant must file a claim within a two-year period from the occurrence of the accidental injury, occupational disablement or death. Failure may bar an award for compensation unless the employer has made advance benefit payments in which event the claim filing requirement is deemed waived. (Sections 20, 28)

CLAIM - (D). A request for disability benefits on a prescribed form DB-450, used if the employee becomes sick or disabled (a) while employed, (b) while on a paid leave of absence or paid vacation, or (c) within four weeks after termination of employment. Completed Claim form DB-450 should be mailed to the employer or his disability benefits insurance carrier. Also, a request for disability benefits on a prescribed form DB-300, used by the employee if he becomes sick or disabled after four weeks of unemployment. Completed claim form DB-300 should be mailed to the Chairman, Workers' Compensation Board, Disability Benefits Bureau, 1949 North Broadway, Albany, New York 12204

COMMITTEE - (A). A responsible person or persons appointed by a court to protect the interests of a mental incompetent. If a committee has not been appointed, the time limitations under the Workers' Compensation Law do not run. (Section 115)

COMMUTED AWARD - (W,V). The actuarially determined value of an award, payable biweekly for a period of future disability, which is changed into a single fixed or gross sum payable into the Aggregate Trust Fund or which forms the basis for a payment to a nonresident alien. (Section 15, Subd. 5-b; Sections 17, 25, 25-b, 27, W.C.L. and Sections 17, 54, V.F.B.L.)

COMPENSATION EXAMINING PHYSICIAN - (A). A physician appointed under Civil Service Regulations to examine claimants for the Workers' Compensation Board. (Section 19)

CONSEQUENTIAL ACCIDENT - (W,V). A second accident resulting from a prior accidental injury which arose out of and in the course of employment. For example, a claimant falling down a flight of stairs at home while using crutches because of a leg injury incurred at work. (Section 2, Subd. 7)

CONTINUING JURISDICTION - (A). The jurisdiction of the Workers' Compensation Board over a workers' compensation claim is continuing, and the Board may from time to time within its discretion, reconsider a claim, change its findings, and either make new awards or modify outstanding awards as in its opinion may appear just. (Section 123)

CONTROVERTED CLAIM - (A). A claim rejected by the carrier on stated grounds. A hearing for the determination of these grounds is set by the Board, and the parties are directed to appear and present their case. (Section 25)

COVERED EMPLOYER - (D). An employer of one or more employees on each of at least 30 days in any calendar year becomes a covered-employer from and after the expiration of four weeks following such 30th day. An employer of personal or domestic employees in a private home becomes a covered employer from and after the expiration of four weeks following employment of four such employees on each of at least 30 days in any calendar year. (Section 202)

# D

DATE CERTAIN - (A). An action taken by a Referee at ahearing in which he arranges for the next hearing of the case on a particular day and time when required witnesses may appear.

DAY OF DISABILITY - (D). Any day on which the employee was prevented from performing work because of disability and for which he has not received his regular remuneration. (Section 201, Subd. 14)

DEFICIENCY COMPENSATION-(W.V.)The difference between the net recovery in a third party action instituted by a claimant on account of a work-connected accidental injury and the amount of workers' compensation payable for such injury, if such amount is larger. Deficiency compensation is payable by the workers' compensation carrier. (Section 29, W.C.L. and Section 20 V.F.B.L.)

DEPENDENCY - (W,V). Death benefits in a fatal injury case may be payable, under certain circumstances, to surviving blind or crippled dependent children over the age of 18, dependent grandchildren, brothers and sisters under the age of 18, and dependent parents and grandparents. These claimants must prove their dependency upon the deceased employee. The regular receipt of contributions by the alleged dependent upon which he relies and which he needs, even if only partially, to sustain him in his customary mode of living, constitutes dependency. The surviving widow, or children under 18 years of age are not required to prove dependency. (Section 15, Subd. 4; Section 16)

DEPOSITION - (A). Evidence of testimony of a witness based upon a series of questions drawn up for the purpose of ascertaining the facts. Depositions are taken where witnesses cannot appear at a hearing before the Board. The questions and answers are part of a proceeding before an official person. (Section 121; Board Rule 19)

DISABILITY (TOTAL)* - (W,V). Disability, medically established, which precludes a claimant from earning any wages. (Section 15, Subds. 1,2)

DISABILITY (PARTIAL) - (W,V). Disability which allows a claimant to engage in some kind of gainful employment. The difference between the claimant's pre-accident earnings and his post-accident earnings is determinative of his reduced earnings rate. In the absence of actual post-accident earnings, the Board may in the interest of justice fix such wage earning capacity as is reasonable. (Section 15, Subds. 5, 5-a)

DISABILITY COMMENCING DURING EMPLOYMENT - (D). The inability of an employee, as the result of injury or sickness not. arising out of and in the course of employment, to perform the regular duties of his employment or the duties of any other employment which his employer may offer him at his regular wages. (Section 201, Subd. 9)

DISABILITY COMMENCING DURING UNEMPLOYMENT - (D). The inability of an employee, as the result of injury or sickness not arising out of and in the course of employment, to perform the duties of any employment for which he is reasonably qualified by training and experience. (Section 201, Subd. 9)

DISABILITY BENEFITS LAW (DEL) - (D). The non-occupational Disability Benefits Law which provides for the payment of benefits to workers out of work because of illness or disabling accidents not connected with their employment.

DOUBLE COMPENSATION - (W). A duplicate award of either compensation or death benefits made on the ground that the injured employee, at the time of the accident, was under the age of 18 years and was permitted or suffered to work in violation of the New York Labor Law or of a rule of the Board of Standards and Appeals. The employer alone and not his carrier is liable for the additional compensation. (Section 14-a)

DOUBLE INDEMNITY - (W). The same as Double Compensation. See explanation appearing immediately above.

# E

EARNING CAPACITY - (W). The ability of a claimant, who has suffered a work-connected disabling injury, to earn wages in the labor market. A claimant's earning capacity is determined by his actual post-accident earnings. In the event he has no actual earnings, the Board may establish a theoretic wage earning capacity which is reasonable on the basis of the record but not in excess of 75% of the claimant's former full time actual earnings. (Section 15, Subd. 5-a)

ELECTION OF REMEDIES - (W). The right of a claimant whose employer was uninsured at time of the accident, to bring a court action against such employer in lieu of claiming workers' compensation (Section 11)

EMPLOYEE CONTRIBUTIONS - (D). An employee may be required to contribute 1/2 of 1% of the first $60.00 of his weekly wage, but not more than 30 cents per week. Where benefits are being provided under a plan approved by the Chairman, contributions of employees may be reduced or eliminated; or may be at a higher rate if the employer and employees have agreed thereto and the employee contribution is reasonably related, in the judgment of the Chairman, to the value of the benefits payable. (Section 209, Subd. 3)

EXCLUSIVENESS OF WORKERS' COMPENSATION REMEDY - (W). The legislature has established the Workers' Compensation Law as the exclusive remedy of an employee and his personal representatives against his employer who has secured workers' compensation. It is the sole recourse that the injured employee, his dependents or representatives have against the employer for injuries or death resulting from a work-connected accident or occupational disease. If an employer who is required to secure workers' compensation insurance fails to do so, his employee if disabled due to a work-connected injury, has the right to elect to either claim workers' compensation or to maintain an action against the uninsured employer for damages. (Section 11)

*For definition of "disability" under the off-the-job Disability Benefits Law see DAY OF DISABILITY, DISABILITY COMMENCING DURING EMPLOYMENT AND DISABILITY COMMENCING DURING UNEMPLOYMENT.

# F

FACIAL DISFIGUREMENT AWARD - (W). An award of compensation for serious permanent facial or head disfigurement.

FINAL ADJUSTMENT (FA) - (W.V). A hearing held in cases involving the loss or loss of use of a member or organ of the body in which the principal issue is the extent of loss or loss of use. (Section 15, Subd. 3)

FUND FOR REOPENED CASES - (W,V). A fund created under the Workers' Compensation Law to assume liability for claims of compensation in certain "stale" cases where specified time limits have elapsed. (Section 25-a, W.C.L. and Section 51, V.F.B.L.)

# G

GENERAL EMPLOYER - (W). The general employer is the regular or parent employer who makes his employee available to a special employer. The general employer usually exercises indirect control and the special employer exercises direct control. If the employee is injured, either employer or both may be liable for the compensation due to the injured employee. (Section 2, Subds. 3,4)

# H

HEARING - (W.V). The Law provides that "No case shall be closed without notice to all parties interested and without giving to all such parties an opportunity to be heard." These "hearings" are held before Referees who hear and determine claims for compensation for the purpose of ascertaining the substantial rights of the parties. (Sections 20, 150)

HEARING - (D). When an employee files with the Chairman a notice that his claim for disability benefits has not been paid, ahearingis held only if requested by the claimant, carrier or employer, or if the issue cannot be resolved administratively.

HEARSAY EVIDENCE - (A). Testimony based upon second-hand information not known directly by the witness but related to him by someone else, constitutes hearsay evidence. It is admissible in a workmen's compensation proceedings. Declarations of a deceased employee concerning the accident are receivable in evidence, and if corroborated by circumstances or other evidence are sufficient to establish the accident and the injury. (Section 118)

## I

IN LINE OF DUTY - (V). Injuries to volunteer firefighters are deemed to be in line of duty if incurred in the course of necessary travel to and from, and work at a fire, alarm of fire or other emergency to which the fire company or any unit thereof has responded, or would be required or authorized to respond and necessary travel during such work. It also covers (1) the performance, pursuant to orders of authorization, including necessary travel directly connected therewith, of duties in the firehouse or elsewhere and the investigation thereof as well as the inspection of property for fire hazards or other dangerous conditions; (2) instruction in fire duties and authorized attendance at a fire school; (3) attendance or work at meetings of the fire department or fire company or any unit thereof; (4) work in connection with the construction, testing, inspection, repair or maintenance of the firehouse and the fixtures, furnishings and equipment thereof, the fire fighting vehicles, fire apparatus and equipment, the fire alarm system, water supply system, fire well, fire cistern or fire suction pool used by the fire department or fire company or other unit thereof; (5) engaging in the inspection of fire fighting vehicles and fire apparatus prior to delivery under a contract of purchase, or performing duties in relation to the delivery thereof; (6) authorized participation in any drill, parade, inspection or review or any competitive tournament, contest or public exhibition in which the fire company or department or any unit thereof is engaged, and attendance at a convention or conference as an authorized delegate of the fire department, company or unit thereof; (7) authorized work in connection with a fund-raising activity of the fire company within the limits of Section 204-a of the General Municipal Law. It also extends to necessary travel to, work in connection with, and necessary travel returning from a call for general ambulance service by a member of an emergency relief squad which has been authorized to furnish such service pursuant to Section 209-b of the General Municipal Law. (Section 3, Subd. 3; Section 5, Volunteer Firefighters' Benefit Law)

INDEXED CLAIM - (W,V). A claim case folder when assembled is referred to as an indexed claim. (Section 141)

INJURY - (D). Injury and sickness mean accidental injury, disease, infection or illness which do not arise out of and in the course of employment. (Section 201, Subd. 8)

## J

JURISDICTION - (W). The Workers' Compensation Board has the right to hear and determine a workmen's compensation case if the employment was located in New York. Proof of the latter would be some of the following contacts with New York State: (1) hiring in New York, (2) work in New York, (3) control of out-of-state employment from New York, (4) residency of claimant in New York, (5) understanding that claimant is to return to New York, following completion of the out-of-state assignment, and (6) occurrence of injury in New York.

JURISDICTION - (D). The Workers' Compensation Board has the right to hear and determine a disability benefits case if the employment is localized in New York; i.e., if it is performed entirely within the State or is performed both within and without the State but that performed without the State is incidental to the employment within the State or is temporary or transitory in nature or consists of isolated transactions; or where the employment is not localized in any state, if the employee's base of operations is in New York; or where there is no base of operations in any state, if the place from which the employment is directed or controlled is in New York; or where the base of operations or place from which the employment is controlled or directed is not in any state in which some part of the service is performed, if the employee's residence is in New York. (Section 201, Subd. 6-c)

## L

LACHES - (A). The failure by a party to assert a right or request the enforcement of a right for a period of time which is unreasonable and unexplained.

LICENSED REPRESENTATIVE - (A). A person other than an attorney who is authorized by the Workers' Compensation Board to represent claimants before the Board, and in some instances, to receive a fee, fixed by the Board, for such services. Also, a person other than an attorney who is authorized by the Workers' Compensation Board to represent self-insurers before the Board. (Sections 24-a, 50(3-b); 225); Board Rule re Licences)

LOST TIME (LT) - (A). The phrase indicates that the claimant's disability has caused lost time and loss of earnings beyond the waiting period (the first seven days of disability). In workmen's compensation cases only, if the disability exceeds 14 days, compensation will be payable from the first day of disability. There is no waiting period in V.F.B.L. cases. (Sections 12, 204-1)

LUMP-SUM NON-SCHEDULE ADJUSTMENT - (W.V). A lump sum paid to a claimant in a non-schedule disability case in which the continuance of disability and of future earning capacity cannot be ascertained with reasonable certainty. Such lump sums must be submitted to the Board for approval after they have been agreed to by the claimant and the carrier. (Section 15, Subd. 5-b)

## M

MEDICAL FEE SCHEDULE - (W,V). The schedule established by the Chairman of the Workers' Compensation Board of charges and fees for medical treatment and care furnished to workmen's compensation claimants. (Section 13, Subd. (a))

MODIFY PREVIOUS AWARD (MPA) - (A). A direction by a presiding Referee or a Board Panel ending, reducing or increasing the workers' compensation previously awarded to the claimant. (Sections 22, 223)

MOTION CALENDAR HEARING - (W,V). A regularly scheduled hearing on a case in which no controversy exists. The notice of hearing contains the proposed decision, and the interested parties are advised that they need not be present at the hearing.

MR-30 - (W,V). Request by Board's Medical Registration Office for decision relative to com-pensability of claim or other issue triable by a Referee, as a prerequisite to taking action on a disputed medical bill. It is instituted following receipt of Form A-1.

## N

NO CLAIM PAPER - (W). A form, paper or correspondence receivedby the Board which does not warrant the indexing of a claim case folder. These papers are filed in the No-Claim File.

NO-DEPENDENCY DEATH CASE - (W,V). A death case in which there are no persons eligible to receive workmen's compensation benefits. In such case, the employer or his insurance carrier pays the funeral expenses, not exceeding $750.00 and $1,000 into the Vocational Rehabilitation Fund, and $1,500 into the Special Fund for Reopened Cases. Under certain circumstances, the $1,500 payment is paid to the Uninsured Employers' Fund instead. (Sections 15(9), 16(1) and 25-a(3), W.C.L. and Sections 15, 51, V.F.B.L.)

NO LOST TIME (NLT) - (W). Claimant has not lost time beyond the waiting period (the first seven days of disability) as a result of his work-connected injuries. (Section 12)

NON-INSURER - (W,D). A subject employer who has failed to provide for the payment of benefits to his employees either under the Workers' Compensation Law or under the Disability Benefits Law. (Sections 50, 220)

NOTICE - (W). Employees who are injured on-the-job must give their employers notice in writing of the occurrence as soon as possible but not later than 30 days thereafter. The Board may excuse the failure to give notice on the ground that notice for some sufficient reason could not have been given or on the ground that the employer had knowledge of the accident or on the ground that the employer had not been prejudiced thereby. In addition, a claim must be filed with the Board within two years. Failure to file a claim may bar an award of compensation unless the employer has made advance payments to the injured worker or has failed to raise the issue at the first hearing at which all parties were present. (Sections 18, 28, 40 and 45)

NOTICE AND PROOF OF CLAIM - (D). Employees who are disabled due to an off-the-job injury or illness must furnish written notice of disability to the employer within fifteen days and must furnish proof of disability (completed by the employee's physician or podiatrist or chiropractor) within twenty days. The prescribed notice and proof are the Claim Forms DB-300 and DB-450. Failure to furnish proof of disability within the 20-day period does not invalidate the claim, but no benefits are required to be paid for any period of disability more than two weeks prior to the date on which the proof was furnished, unless it be shown to the satisfaction of the Chairman that it had not been reasonably possible to furnish it within the prescribed time and that it was done as soon as possible. However, no benefits shall be paid unless the proof of disability was furnished within twenty-six weeks after the commencement of disability.

NOTICE - (V). Under the Volunteer Firemen's Benefit Law, notice of injury or death must be given by the injured volunteer fireman or his dependents within 90 days after the injury or death. (See Q. and A. 14 under the Volunteer Firefighters' Benefit Law)

## O

OCCUPATIONAL DISEASE - (W,V). A disease arising from the conditions to which all employees of a class are subject and which produces the disease as a natural incident of a particular occupation as distinguished from and exceeding the hazard and risk of ordinary employment. A disease does not become an occupational disease merely because it is contracted on the employer's premises'in the course of the employment; it must be one which is commonly regarded as natural to, inhering in, or an incident of the work in question. There must be a recognizable link between the disease and some distinctive feature of the claimant's job. (Sections 3(2), 37, 49-a)

## P

PLAN BENEFIT - (D). Disability Benefits provided under a plan or agreement accepted by the Chairman. An employer, unilaterally or as a result of collective bargaining may provide plan benefits, i.e. benefits that differ from statutory benefits in amounts of benefits paid, duration of benefits and waiting period. Plan benefits may also include hospital, surgical and/or medical care benefits. (Section 211)

PODIATRY FEE SCHEDULE - (W.V). The schedule established by the Chairman of the Workers' Compensation Board of charges and fees for podiatric treatment and care furnished to workers' compensation claimants. (Section 13-K)

PRESUMPTIONS - (W). In a claim for workers' compensation, it is presumed in the absence of substantial evidence to the contrary, that the claim falls within the Law; that sufficient notice was given; that the injury was not occasioned by the willful intention of the injured employee to bring about the injury or death of himself or another; and that death did not result solely from the intoxication of the injured employee. (Sections 21, 47)

PROTRACTED HEALING PERIOD - (W,V). In case of temporary total disability and permanent partial disability both resulting from the same schedule injury, if the period of temporary total disability continues for a longer period than the normal healing period as set forth in Section 15, Subd. 4-a, the period of temporary total disability in excess of such normal healing period is added to the schedule award. (Section 15, Subd. 4-a, W.C.L. and Section 9, V.F.B.L.)

PROOF OF CLAIM - (D). See "Notice and Proof of Claim".

## R

RED SEAL SUMMONS - (W,D). A summons issued by the Board requiring an employer to appear at the Board or to furnish information by mail regarding his compliance with either the Workmen's Compensation Law or the Disability Benefits Law.

REDUCED EARNINGS (RE) - (W). A compensation rate based on the claimant's reduced earnings or his reduced earning capacity due to a condition related to his compensable work-connected injury. (Section 15)

REFEREE - (A). A quasi-judicial officer appointed by the Workers' Compensation Board to hear and determine claims and to conduct such hearings and investigations and make such orders, decisions, and determinations as may be required in the adjudication of the claims. His decision is deemed the decision of the Board unless the Board modifies or rescinds such decision. (Section 150)

REFORMATION OF INSURANCE POLICY - (A). The Workers' Compensation Board has the power to reform or rectify an insurance policy whenever the policy fails through fraud or mutual mistake to reflect the real agreement or actual intention of the parties.

REHABILITATION - (W,V). The process of restoring injured workers to productive employment through physical means, medical procedures, vocational retraining, selective placement, and social readjustment. Rehabilitation is an integral part of the medical care and other services furnished a claimant under the Law. (Section 13, Subd. a)

REMARRIAGE AWARD - (W,V). An award of two years' compensation paid in a lump sum, to the surviving widow or surviving dependent widower of a fatally injured worker upon her or his remarriage. (Section 16, Subd. 2)

REOPENED CASE - (A). A case which has been closed by a Referee or the Board, and is subsequently made active again to determine the claimant's eligibility for benefits. (Sections 22, 23 and 224)

REOPENED CASES FUND - (W,V). When an application to reopen a closed case is made more than seven years from the date of injury and more than three years from the date of the last payment of compensation, liability for any additional workers' compensation awarded in the case is imposed against the Reopened Cases Fund. The latter is financed through payments in non-dependency death cases and through assessments made periodically against all carriers. (Section 25-a, W.C.L. and Section 51, V.F.B.L.)

REQUEST FOR REIMBURSEMENT - (A). A request by an employer for reimbursement of wages paid to an employee for a period during which he was eligible to receive workers' compensation or disability benefits. Also, a request by a Compensation carrier for reimbursement out of the Special Disability Fund (Second Injury Fund); and a request by a Disability Benefits carrier for reimbursement of benefits paid to a claimant while his workmen's compensation case was being litigated. (Section 15(8), 25, 206(2) )

REVIEW ASSESSMENT - (A). An assessment made by the Board where the decision of a Referee is affirmed by the Board upon review. A carrier or employer seeking such a review is assessed $25; all other parties may be assessed $5. (Section 151)

## S

SCHEDULE LOSS - (W,V). The number of weeks of compensation payable for permanent partial disability due to the loss or loss of use of certain members of the body or organs as listed in Section 15, Subd. 3 of the Law. (Section 10, V.F.B.L.)

SECOND INJURY FUND - (W). A Fund, technically known as the Special Disability Fund, created to encourage employers to hire physically handicapped persons by protecting them against a disproportionate liability in the event of subsequent employment injury. At the same time, the Second Injury Law assures the injured handicapped worker full workers' compensation benefits. (Section 15, Subd. 8)

SECOND INJURY LAW - (W). This Law is designed to encourage the employment of handicapped workers by limiting the liability of an employer in the event they sustain further permanent disability due to work-connected injury. (Section 15, Subd. 8) See also Second Injury Fund, above.

SELF-INSURANCE - (W,D,V). A method by which an employer or group of employers may secure the payment of workers' compensation or disability benefits to his or its employees by depositing securities or a surety bond in an amount required by the Chairman of the Workers' Compensation Board. This method is in lieu of purchasing insurance from an insurance company. (Sections 50, 211, W.C.L. and Section 3, Subd. 13, V.F.B.L.)

SICKNESS - (D). See "Injury".

SLOW-STARTING OCCUPATIONAL DISEASE - (W). The Law identifies the diseases in this category as those caused by compressed air illness or its sequelae, or by latent or delayed pathological bone, blood or lung changes or malignancies due to occupational exposure or contact with arsenic, benzol, beryllium, zirconium, cadmium, chrome, lead or fluorine or to exposure to X-rays, radium, ionizing radiation or radioactive substances. (Sections 28, 40)

SPECIAL FUNDS - (A). These are Funds specifically created in the Workers' Compensation and Disability Benefits Laws. There are ten such Funds. They are designed mainly to assure payment of benefits to claimants. In certain instances, (Section 15, Subd. 8, and Section 25-a) the liability of the employer for compensation to his injured worker is transferred to the Fund, and the employer is relieved in part or in whole of such liability. (Sections 15, Subd. 9, 25-b, 26-a, 107, 109-d, 214, 319)

SPECIAL FUNDS CONSERVATION COMMITTEE - (W). A committee created in accordance with Se'ction 15, Subd. 8 and Section 25-a of the Law to defend claims made against the Special Funds created under those sections.

SPECIAL FUND FOR DISABILITY BENEFITS - (D). Administered by the Chairman and used to pay benefits to (1) unemployed claimants whose disability commences more than four weeks following termination of employment; (2) employees of covered employers who have failed to comply with the requirement to have disability benefits insurance; and (3) employees of a covered employer whose insurance carrier fails to'pay the benefits. (Section 214)

STATE INSURANCE FUND - (A). A Fund created by the State pursuant to Section 76 of the Law for the purpose of insuring employers in the field of workmen's compensation, disability benefits and volunteer firemen's benefit insurance.

STATUTE OF LIMITATIONS - (A). Statutory enactments that prescribe the periods within which actions may be brought upon certain claims or within which certain rights may be enforced. Some of the statutes of limitations in the Workers' Compensation Law are:

Section 15, Subd. 8. In a Second Injury Law case, the employer or carrier must file notice of claim for reimbursement from the Special Disability Fund within 104 weeks after the date of disability or death, or in a reopened case, no later than the determination of permanency upon such reopening.

Section 18. Written notice of injury or death must be given to the employer within 30 days after the accident causing such injury. (Note: The Board may excuse the failure to do so on specified grounds.)
Section 23. An application for Board review must be made within 30 days after notice of the filing of the award or decision of the Referee. An appeal to the Appellate Division, Third Department, must be taken within 30 days after notice of the Board decision.

Section 25-a. An application for compensation may be made against the Reopened Cases Fund after a lapse of seven years from the date of injury or death and also a lapse of three years from the date of the last payment of compensation. Awards made against the Reopened Cases Fund are not retroactive for a period of more than two years immediately preceding the date of filing of the application for reopening.

Section 28. The right to claim compensation is barred unless a claim for compensation is filed with the Chairman of the Board within two years after the accident. An employer is deemed to have waived the bar of this statute unless the objection to the failure to file the claim within two years is raised at the first hearing on such claim at which all parties in interest are present. Also, no case in which an advance payment is made is barred by the failure to file a claim. (IMPORTANT; The Board may not excuse the failure to file a claim within the two-year period.)

Section 40. The time limitation between contraction of an occupational disease and disablement therefrom is 12 months, but such time limitation is inapplicable in the slow-starting diseases enumerated in the Law. It is also inapplicable in the case of an employee who has continued in the same employment with the same employer from the time of contracting the disease up to the time of his disablement thereby.

Section 54, Subd. 5. No contract of workers' compensation insurance may be cancelled within the time limits in such contract, prior to its expiration, until at least 10 days after notice of cancellation is filed in the office of the Chairman and also served on the employer.

Section 110. Every employer shall report within 10 days the occurrence of an accident resulting in personal injury which causes a loss of time beyond the day of the occurrence or which requires medical treatment beyond ordinary first aid or more than two medical treatments by a person rendering first aid.

Section 115. No limitation of time shall run as against any person who is mentally incompetent or a minor so long as he has no committee or guardian.

Section 123. No awards of compensation or death benefits may be made after a lapse of 18 years from the date of injury or death and a lapse of 8 years from the date of the last payment of compensation.

---

All sectional references are to the Workmen's Compensation Law unless otherwise indicated

Section 217. In a Disability Benefits Law case, notice of disability must be furnished to the employer within fifteen days; and proof of claim, within twenty days. Late filing of proof of claim does not invalidate claim - (See "Notice and Proof of Claim"). No benefits are payable unless proof of disability is furnished within twenty-six weeks after start of disability. In the case of an unemployed claimant, the disability must commence within 26 weeks following termination of employment. (Section 207)

STATUTORY BENEFITS - (D). Under the Disability Benefits Law, the statutory weekly benefit rate is 50% of the employee's average weekly wage; maximum $95.00 per week, minimum $20.00 per week or average weekly wage if latter is less than $20.00. Statutory disability benefits are payable, after a 7-day waiting period, for a maximum period of twenty-six weeks in any fifty-two consecutive weeks or during any one period of disability. (Section 204, Subd. 2, Section 205, Subd. 1)

STATUTORY COVERAGE - (D). The benefits specified in the Disability Benefits Law which an employer must provide for his employees unless the Board has approved an employer's plan which provides benefits which are different but at least as favorable as the statutory benefits. In the case of an existing obligated plan which was in existence prior to April 13, 1949, the benefits provided may be less than statutory. (Article 9)

STATUS QUO ANTE - (W,V). The term signifies that a claimant's health has returned to what it was before the occurrence of the accient.

SUBPOENA - (A). A legal writ commanding a designated person to appear and give testimony at a workmen's compensation hearing under penalty for failure to do so. The Chairman, Board Members, Referees, officers of the Board designated by the Chairman and any attorney may sign and issue a subpoena, or a subpoena duces tecum, the latter requiring the production of records. (Sections 119, 142(3), 231)

SUBROGATION - (A). The assignment of a cause of action against a third party by the claimant to the carrier. Failure of a claimant to commence a third party action, if cause therefor exists, within the period of time specified in Section 29 (in a Workmen's Compensation case) and 227 (in a Disability Benefits case) operates as an assignment of the cause of action to the carrier liable for the payment of compensation or disability benefits provided that proper notice of such subrogation is given to the claimant. (Sections 29, 227, W.C.L.; Section 20, V.F.B.L.)

## T

TEMPORARY REDUCED EARNINGS RATE (TRE) - (W). A temporary reduced earnings rate of compensation pending adjudication of the actual amount of reduced earnings or the determination of the claimant's reduced wage earning capacity. (Section 15, Subds. 5, 5-a)

TENTATIVE RATE (TR) - (W). The tentative rate of compensation pending final adjudication of the issues relating to rate. (Sections 14, 15)

THIRD PARTY SETTLEMENT - (A). When an employee is injured by the negligence or wrong of a party he may sue such party other than the employer or a fellow employee, if injured in the course of employment. The carrier which has paid compensation or disability benefits to the employee has a lien against any recovery in the third party action. A settlement of such action is called a third party settlement. (Sections 29, 227, W.C.L.; Section 20, V.F.B.L.)

## U

UNINSURED EMPLOYERS' FUND - (W). A special fund which provides for the payment of workmen's compensation in cases where the employer was not insured nor self-insured, and he has defaulted in the payment of workmen's compensation. (Section 26-a)

## W

WAGE EXPECTANCY - (W). The wages of a claimant, who is a minor at the time of the occurrence of the accident, are presumed to increase under normal conditions, and the Board may consider that fact in establishing the claimant's compensation rate if his injuries are permanent. (Section 14, Subd. 5)

WAGES - (W,D). The money rate at which employment with an employer is recompensed under the contract of hiring with the employer and shall include the reasonable value of board, rent, housing, lodging or similar advantage received under the contract of hiring. (Section 2, Subd. 9, Section 201, Subd. 12)

WAITING PERIOD - (W,D). Neither workmen's compensation nor disability benefits are allowable for the first seven days of disability, except that (1) in the case of an on-the-job accident, if disability exceeds 14 days, cash compensation is allowable from the date of the disability; and (2) in the case of disability benefits, (a) the sick unemployed, receiving unemployment insurance at the time they become sick, are not subjected to a waiting period, and (b) under a plan or agreement accepted by the Chairman, the waiting period may be less than 7 days or eliminated entirely. There is no "waiting period" in V.F.B.L. cases. (Sections 12, 204, 2D7, 211)